D1623976

Tales from the

WISCONSIN
BADGERS

JUSTIN DOHERTY

Foreword by **Barry Alvarez**

www.SportsPublishingLLC.com

ISBN: 1-58261-408-3

Publishers: Peter L. Bannon and Joseph J. Bannon Sr.
Senior managing editor: Susan M. Moyer
Acquisitions editor: Mike Pearson
Developmental editor: Regina D. Sabbia
Art director: K. Jeffrey Higgerson
Dust jacket design: Kenneth J. O'Brien
Interior layout: Kenneth J. O'Brien
Imaging: Kenneth J. O'Brien
Photo editor: Erin Linden-Levy
Vice president of sales and marketing: Kevin King
Media and promotions managers: Nick Obradovich (regional),
    Randy Fouts (national), Maurey Williamson (print)

Printed in the United States of America

Sports Publishing L.L.C.
804 North Neil Street
Champaign, IL 61820

Phone: 1-877-424-2665
Fax: 217-363-2073
www.SportsPublishingLLC.com

*For my family, friends and
Badger fans everywhere*

CONTENTS

ACKNOWLEDGMENTS

I did the writing, but this book would not have been possible without the assistance, encouragement and support of a great many people.

Thanks, first, to my wife, Martha, and our daughter, Erin. Their unfailing support during the many hours this project required was very meaningful and much appreciated.

To UW associate athletic director Steve Malchow, a friend and professional colleague (actually, my boss) for 11 years, for allowing me to take on this project and for his willingness to edit and offer advice.

To Matt Lepay, the "Voice of the Badgers;" Mike Lucas, longtime Madison columnist and color commentator for Badger sports; Dennis Chaptman of University Communications; Allison Wachs, a former student associate in our office who is now a researcher at ESPN; and associate athletic director John Chadima— thanks so much for taking the time to read, edit, and make suggestions.

The following individuals graciously allowed me the time to interview them in my effort to uncover some untold stories or to simply relive some really good ones. I appreciate the time each of these people gave to me: Barry Alvarez, Doug Beard, Brooks Bollinger, Wendell Bryant, Father Mike Burke, Tom Butler, John Chadima, John Dettmann, Lee Evans, Jeff Horton, Jim Hueber, Kevin Kluender, Mike Leckrone, Matt Lepay, Mike Lucas, Mike Mahnke, Steve Malchow, Bill Marek, Jeff Nelson, Scott Nelson, Pat O'Connor, John Palermo, Joe Panos, Mark Peeler, Jamie Pollard, Pat Richter, Will Roleson, Joe Rudolph, Jim Sorgi, Brian White, and Bernie Wyatt.

Greg Bond's fascinating research on Wisconsin's African-American athletic history, which is available at www.uwbadgers.com, was very helpful.

I am grateful to David Stluka for the use of his excellent photography, not only on the cover, but also on the inside pages of this book.

Thanks to Mike Pearson of Sports Publishing LLC, for encouraging me to get involved with this book, and to my editor, Gina Sabbia, a Wisconsin graduate who helped guide me through the process.

Finally, thanks to my parents, who always encouraged and supported my interests. My father passed away while I was writing this book, but I hope he would have liked the final product.

FOREWORD

It doesn't seem possible that almost 16 years have passed since I came to Madison as head football coach at Wisconsin. I can still clearly remember my first meeting with Pat Richter, holding my first press conference to announce that I had accepted the position and then heading out immediately to start recruiting.

In fact, we signed many players that winter who helped form the nucleus of our first Big Ten and Rose Bowl championship team in 1993. Those players, and the hundreds who came after them, represent some of my most special memories. It is the relationships you form with the young men, as well as fellow coaches, staff members and fans, that make my job so rewarding.

In addition to trying to help our players mature, receive an education, and become productive parts of our society, however, we are also trying to win football games. The big games we have won, the great performances of our players, our fantastic fans at Camp Randall Stadium—those things will stick with me forever.

There are so many great memories. Our win over Ohio State in 1992 was our first over a nationally ranked opponent. The trip to Tokyo, clinching the 1993 Big Ten title and winning the Rose Bowl. The win at sixth-ranked Penn State that stopped the Nittany Lions' 20-game winning streak in 1995. The "Ron Dayne Game" against Iowa in 1999 and our back-to-back conference and Rose Bowl crowns in 1998 and 1999. Lee Evans's 79-yard touchdown reception against No. 3 Ohio State at Camp Randall in 2003. These are just a few of the highlights that come to my mind.

It is not just about the games, either. As I mentioned earlier, it's the relationships. It makes me so proud to see our former players doing well in their chosen fields of work and in their personal lives. I enjoy them returning to Camp Randall, even if it is just for a few minutes to say hello.

But Badger football is also about a long history of players, games, coaches and fans that were here long before I ever got to

Madison. The stories of Pat O'Dea, Elroy "Crazylegs" Hirsch, Pat Richter, Rufus Ferguson, Billy Marek and Al Toon. Memorable games like the 1942 win over No. 1-ranked Ohio State, the 1963 Rose Bowl, the 1981 season-opening victory over Michigan. It's all part of Badger football.

I know you'll enjoy reading about just some the players, coaches, staff and games that form what is a rich and colorful football tradition at Wisconsin.

GO BADGERS!

—Barry Alvarez,
Director of Athletics and Head Football Coach

CHAPTER ONE

1889-1919

Wisconsin actually started playing football in 1889, but several significant things happened for the program as it proceeded through the 1890s. First off, Wisconsin won quite a bit. The UW was 56-18-3 during its first full decade of play, including being the winner of the first two Big Ten (then Western) Conference titles under the direction of head coach Phil King.

Speaking of the Western Conference, in 1896 Wisconsin joined Chicago, Illinois, Michigan, Minnesota, Northwestern, and Purdue as charter members of what later became the Big Ten.

Wisconsin's famed fight song, "On Wisconsin," was introduced in 1909 and later during this period Wisconsin had its first All-American (Robert "Butts" Butler) named. Others like Howard "Cub" Buck and Arlie Mucks Sr. starred for the Badgers, and in 1917 Camp Randall Stadium opened.

Why They Call It Camp Randall

Few college football facilities in the United States are as unique and steeped in history as Wisconsin's Camp Randall Stadium.

Prior to the Civil War, the State Agricultural Society owned the site and used it for state fairs. When the war began, however, the grounds were turned over to the government to be used as a military training center. Some 70,000 soldiers trained at the camp, which also featured a hospital and a prison for Confederate soldiers on its grounds.

The state fair returned following the war (General U.S. Grant referred to the transformation as "a symbol of beating the spears of war into the plowshares of peace"), but eventually moved to Milwaukee. Rather than put the land up for sale, the state, at the urging of Civil War veterans, gave the land to the University in 1893. Veterans favored naming it Camp Randall instead of Randall Field in honor of the site's function during the Civil War (it was

An early view of Camp Randall Stadium and its grounds
Photo courtesy of UW Athletic Communications

originally named for Alexander Randall, the state's first wartime governor).

A small part of the area was set aside as a memorial park in 1911. One entryway into the park is the Memorial Arch, built by the state to honor the 70,000 troops who trained there.

The Camp Randall grounds contained a stadium by 1913, but its stands were made of wood. A sizeable section of the wooden bleachers collapsed at the Badgers' 20-3 win over Minnesota in 1915, injuring 20 people. That prompted the construction of what is now Camp Randall Stadium.

The original stadium, with a capacity of 10,000, was started with a $20,000 grant from the state. Though the first game played at the new facility was on October 6, 1917, against Beloit, it was officially dedicated when the Badgers defeated Minnesota 10-7 on Homecoming (November 3) that year.

The Badgers Are Born

The first "official" Wisconsin football game took place in Milwaukee against the Calumet Club of Milwaukee on November 23, 1889.

The *Milwaukee Sentinel* declared (somewhat prophetically in its description of the UW student fans) on the day of the contest: "There promises to be plenty of excitement, as the University team will be accompanied by a delegation of students, each of whom will bring two sound lungs with him."

The newspaper's colorful description of the "Madison University" football team's 27-0 loss included an acknowledgment that the "Milwaukee men were assisted considerably in their victory by the umpire, who appeared to be rather hard on the university boys in several of his decisions."

The two teams concluded the event when the Milwaukee team "gave three cheers for Madison, and Madison returned the compliment with three cheers for Milwaukee."

First Night Game

Wisconsin's first night football game was played against the Carlisle (Pennsylvania) Indians (the great Jim Thorpe later attended the school) in the Chicago Coliseum on December 19, 1896.

Newspaper stories before the game indicated Wisconsin, which featured legendary kicker Pat O'Dea and won the inaugural Western Conference title that season, felt quite confident in its chances against the Indians. "[First-year head coach] Phil King will leave for the east tomorrow after the victory which he confidently expects has been properly celebrated," wrote the *Wisconsin State Journal* the day before the contest. The paper also reported that President-elect William McKinley would attend the game.

Wisconsin, however, lost to Carlisle, 18-8. The Indians erased an 8-6 deficit in the second half with a pair of touchdowns. The indoor game reportedly went off without a hitch, although there was one delay when a punted ball landed high on one of the girders that supported the roof of the facility. The *Chicago Tribune* wrote that the ball remained stuck, "until a boy in the gallery climbed out and dropped it to the ground."

One of Wisconsin's key players was lineman J.F.A. "Sunny" Pyre, who was reported to have battled Bemus and Hawley Pierce, a pair of Seneca Indians, ferociously that night. Pyre later became an English professor at UW-Madison, as well as the school's faculty representative to the Big Ten Conference.

The headline of the *Tribune's* story about the game stated: "Indians Get The Scalps." That was followed by a lead paragraph that read: "Scions of the aborigines, representing eight tribes of North American Indians, left the Coliseum last night, after one of the most hotly contested games of football ever witnessed, with the scalps of eleven Wisconsin men dangling at their belts."

"Varsity"

College football is a sport rich in traditions and one of the most well-known traditions at Wisconsin home football games is the playing of "Varsity" and the arm-waving that adds a visual element to the nostalgic feeling that comes with singing the University's alma mater.

The song was originally written (its Latin translation was "Domine Salvam Fac") in 1853 by French composer Charles Gounod as a part of a church service. Then, in 1898, a music instructor at the University, Henry Dyke Sleeper, wrote the words and arranged the music for what was then called "Varsity Toast."

Former UW Band director Ray Dvorak is responsible for the addition of the arm waving that complements the tune. Dvorak, while an assistant band director at Illinois, accompanied the Fighting Illini football team to a game at the University of Pennsylvania. According to Dvorak, the Penn students sang their alma mater after the game and at the end of the song, "waved their derbies in the air to the words 'Hail, Hail, Hail.'"

Dvorak brought the concept to Madison and instituted it first as a salute to University president Glenn Frank, who had finished speaking at a mid-year commencement ceremony.

Popularizing the Forward Pass

Names like Ameche, Ferguson, Marek, Dayne, and Davis underline Wisconsin's tradition of great running backs. It is somewhat ironic, then, that a Badger football pioneer is credited with the first effective use of the forward pass.

Eddie Cochems starred for the Badgers as an end in 1898 and 1899 before moving to halfback and teaming with Albert "Norsky" Larson and Earl "Keg" Driver to form a feared backfield the next two years.

Cochems was a thorn in the side of legendary Coach Amos Alonzo Stagg's University of Chicago Maroons. He scored a pair of touchdowns in a 39-5 win over Chicago in 1900 and then tallied three times (including a 100-yard kickoff return) the next year in a 35-0 Wisconsin victory over the Maroons.

Cochems, a native of Sturgeon Bay, Wisconsin, went on to coach at St. Louis University from 1906-1908. It was during his years at St. Louis that he originated the recently legalized forward pass. In fact, legendary Notre Dame coach Knute Rockne later credited Cochems with popularizing the forward pass, and his assertion can be validated by a 67-yard pass from St. Louis's Bradbury Robinson to John Schneider in a 1906 game against Kansas.

The Kangaroo Kicker

The exploits of one of Wisconsin's true football legends are more than 100 years old now, but the story of Pat O'Dea reads as well now as it did then.

Known as the "Kangaroo Kicker," O'Dea was born in Melbourne, Australia, and came to Madison in the spring of 1896 to join his brother, Andy, who had come to Wisconsin as varsity crew coach the year before. Pat enrolled at UW-Madison in the fall.

A standout rugby player as a teenager in Australia, Pat O'Dea was reportedly watching the Wisconsin football team practice when a ball rolled in his direction. O'Dea returned the ball by kicking it the length of the field, amazing all onlookers and convincing the players and coaches that they needed him on the team.

O'Dea launched an 85-yard punt in his first appearance against Lake Forest in 1896. He was a fullback for the next three seasons, earning All-America recognition twice from Walter Camp. Among his remarkable feats were punts of 110 and 100 yards, respectively, against Minnesota in 1897 and Yale in 1899; drop-kicked field goals of 62 and 60 yards, respectively, against Northwestern in 1898 (in a blizzard) and Minnesota in 1899; and a 100-yard touchdown run against Beloit in 1899.

Following his playing days at Wisconsin, O'Dea coached at Notre Dame and Missouri before moving to San Francisco to practice law. He mysteriously disappeared, however, and friends searched for his whereabouts for years. In 1934 the *San Francisco Chronicle* reported that it had found O'Dea living under another

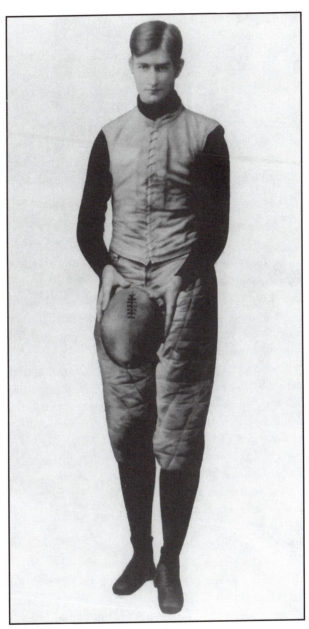

Pat O'Dea, the famed "Kangaroo Kicker"
Photo courtesy of UW Athletic Communications

name (Charles Mitchell) and working for a lumber company in Westwood, California.

O'Dea's friends back in Wisconsin did not believe the story until Henry J. McCormick, the late *Wisconsin State Journal* sports editor, and O'Dea's teammate, Earl "Slam" Anderson, questioned the former kicking star via telegram. O'Dea's responses confirmed his reappearance.

The UW Department of Athletics celebrated O'Dea's return by inviting him back to Madison for the 1934 Homecoming game against Illinois. O'Dea was inducted into the National Football Foundation's College Hall of Fame in 1962.

"On, Minnesota?"

Knowing that the University of Minnesota was looking for a new football fight song, William Purdy, a composer from Chicago, had decided to submit a piece of music he had written. Wisconsin fans can thank Purdy's roommate, Carl Beck (a Wisconsin alumnus), for convincing his friend not to do that.

Beck, who wrote the lyrics, had his friend contribute the song to Wisconsin and it was introduced in 1909. "On, Wisconsin" has, of course, gone on to become one of the most famous college fight songs in the nation. Here are the lyrics:

On Wisconsin, On Wisconsin
Plunge right through that line
Run the ball clear down the field, boys
Touchdown sure this time …
On Wisconsin, On Wisconsin
Fight on for her fame
Fight, fellows, Fight, Fight Fight
We'll win this game!

Purdy sold the copyright to the song in 1918 for less than $100. Years later, "On, Wisconsin," which John Philip Sousa called "the finest of college marching songs," became the official state song. Its rights actually were transferred to former Beatle Paul McCartney in the 1980s when the rock star purchased the music catalog (which included "On, Wisconsin") owned by Melrose Music. Pop star Michael Jackson purchased the Melrose catalog from McCartney but, according to UW Band Director Mike Leckrone, the song is now considered to be in the public domain.

The First All-American

The first first-team All-American in Wisconsin football history was Robert "Butts" Butler, who made the *Collier's* team, chosen by Walter Camp, in 1912. That Wisconsin team was the last one to finish a season undefeated.

Butler, originally from Glen Ridge, New Jersey, was one of 11 starters to play the entire game in Wisconsin's 14-0 victory over Minnesota in 1912. He went on to play professionally with the Canton Bulldogs and is a member of the National Football Foundation Hall of Fame.

While with Canton, Butler played against the legendary Jim Thorpe. "I thought a lot of that stuff the sports writers said about Thorpe must have been overdone," Butler said. "I thought he couldn't be that good. But he was that good, the greatest football player I've ever seen."

A Tackle Called "Cub"

Wisconsin was just 11-8-2 during the three (1913-1915) seasons that Howard E. "Cub" Buck played tackle, but the team's record did little to diminish the accomplishments of one of the great players of the pre-World War I era.

Midwesterners were in disbelief when Walter Camp named Buck a second-team All-American in 1915. Legend had it that Camp's first team was to play the second team, but when the first-teamers heard Buck was on the second team they refused to play, claiming he was a one-man team.

Buck, who made half of Wisconsin's tackles in 1915, even garnered the support of writer Ring Lardner, who was with the

Chicago Tribune at the time. "Them Wisconsins have got one demon tho," wrote Lardner. "They call him Cub and he's a bear. His other name is Buck, and he sure can. I've seen all these here teams this fall and he's the best tackle I ever seen."

Buck went on to play for Curly Lambeau in Green Bay from 1921-1925. He later became the first football coach at the University of Miami.

The Discus Champ

Arlie Mucks Sr. was a first-team All-America guard on the 1914 Wisconsin football team, but he may be better known for his track and field exploits.

A native of Oshkosh, Wisconsin, Mucks made the 1912 United States Olympic Team that competed at the Olympic Summer Games in Stockholm, Sweden. Mucks, whose fellow American Olympians included Jim Thorpe, Avery Brundage, and George S. Patton (later a legendary World War II general), placed second in the discus.

He went on to set the world record in the discus and won the national championship in the shot and discus three times. Mucks later became a professor at UW-Madison and a national leader in agricultural extension.

CHAPTER TWO

The 1920s

Often called the "Golden Age of Sports" because of the exploits of legends like Babe Ruth, Bobby Jones, Jack Dempsey, and Notre Dame's Four Horsemen, the 1920s was a decade of ups and downs for the Badger football program. Wisconsin had four different head coaches during that time and finished second in the Big Ten on three occasions. The Badgers, however, also twice slipped to 10th place in league play and tied for ninth one other time.

Eckersall Escapes

Thanks to the efforts of Wisconsin football team captain Marty Below, several of his teammates and UW head coach Jack Ryan, Walter Eckersall made it out of Camp Randall Stadium alive—but just barely.

Eckersall was officiating the Badgers' 1923 home game with Michigan. Wisconsin fans, incensed at a second-quarter call that allowed the Wolverines to score the only touchdown in a 6-3 victory over the Badgers, gathered at the gate through which Eckersall was to leave the field.

As Eckersall made his way through the crowd, he was struck by an unidentified fan, who was not charged and was released outside the gate at Eckersall's request.

Fans crowded toward Eckersall as Below and his teammates held them off so the official could be taken to a corner of the field. Eventually, Ryan got Eckersall into his car and drove him to Milwaukee.

Live on the Radio

Coach Jack Ryan's 1924 Badger squad took part in what is believed to be the first live radio broadcast originating from a football stadium.

Edwin L. "Ty" Tyson approached Michigan athletic director Fielding Yost about broadcasting the Wolverines-Badgers game, but Yost, concerned about hurting attendance, was somewhat reluctant. Yost ultimately agreed to Tyson's proposal on the condition that the game would be a sellout. That was all but guaranteed after a controversial 6-3 Michigan win at Camp Randall Stadium the year before had heightened interest in the 1924 contest in Ann Arbor.

"It sure was a sellout," Tyson later recalled. "Doc [Holland] and I had to pay to get in just like everyone else."

Tyson and Leonard "Doc" Holland described the action from the east end zone stands of Michigan's Ferry Field on October 25. Detroit's WWJ Radio, one of the first commercial radio stations in the United States, carried the Wolverines' 21-0 victory over the Badgers.

Below's Blind Date

The next time the Badgers travel to Ann Arbor to face Michigan, they will most likely board a chartered airplane Friday evening, arrive in Michigan an hour later and be back in Madison a few hours after the end of the game on Saturday.

Team travel was not, however, always like that. If it were, Marty Below never would have met his wife, Florence.

Below, a member of the National Football Foundation's College Football Hall of Fame, played one season at UW-Madison in 1918 before returning home to Oshkosh, Wisconsin, and attending college there for two years. He went back to Madison and was eligible to play football for the Badgers in 1922.

Wisconsin ventured to Ann Arbor for a November 18 matchup with the Wolverines, who were hosting their homecoming game. In those days the team traveled by train, leaving Thursday evening and arriving on Friday. "We'd have a workout and get plenty of rest before the game on Saturday," Below told the *Milwaukee Journal* in 1977. The team would then travel Saturday night to arrive back in Madison on Sunday.

Despite a 13-6 defeat at the hands of the Wolverines that day, the trip was not a total loss for Below, who had a blind date set up after the game at a dance at Michigan's student union. Below was, in his own words, "all banged up," with a patch on one of his eyes.

"I think that's what caught her attention, and things blossomed from there," he said.

Below and Florence were married in 1925 and later became the parents of three children. Marty Below, an All-America tackle in 1923, died in 1984.

The Greatest Lineman

It was a letter full of playful good will and good wishes, birthday salutations from one old friend to another. It also was validation of Marty Below's greatness as a football player.

Below, a tackle, earned consensus All-America honors as Wisconsin's captain in 1923. A two-time, first-team All-Big Ten selection, he went on to be elected to the National Football Foundation's College Football Hall of Fame.

As Below's friends were putting together plans to celebrate his 78th birthday, a letter arrived from an old friend and football rival. The note recounted playing days from years gone by and complimentarily referred to Below as a great competitor and a gentleman.

"Marty and I have been friends for many years, and you can believe me when I say that he was the Greatest Lineman I ever played against in College," the letter's author wrote toward the end.

It was signed by the legendary Harold "Red" Grange, who starred as a running back in college at Illinois before joining head coach George Halas's Chicago Bears.

Badgers Bury Hawkeyes in Blizzard

Head coach George Little's 1925 Badgers earned one of the school's great wins of that era when they knocked off first-place Iowa, in Iowa City, 6-0 in a raging blizzard.

"It's the greatest victory I have ever had anything to do with," Little told the *Wisconsin State Journal* after the game.

Wisconsin, which did not throw a pass in the game, got a one-yard touchdown run from "Red" Kreuz in the fourth quarter to account for all the scoring.

Newspaper accounts of the game talk of ankle-deep snow on the field.

"Big Reb"

Wisconsin finished the 1929 season with a 4-5 overall record and, in fact, went four straight games without scoring in consecutive losses to Northwestern, Notre Dame, Iowa, and Purdue. But the season was memorable if only for the performance of Harold "Big Reb" Rebholz in the season finale against Minnesota.

The Badgers dropped a 13-12 decision to the Golden Gophers on a typical late fall afternoon in Minneapolis. It was Rebholz's battle with Minnesota's legendary Bronko Nagurski, however, that drew most of the attention.

Both Rebholz and Nagurski played on both sides of the ball, keying on each other and tackling each other in bone-jarring fashion. Offensively, Rebholz carried the ball 12 times for 46 yards, while Nagurski gained 39 yards on 16 carries.

Nagurski went on to call Rebholz the greatest defensive player he had faced in college. "Rebholz had an uncanny knack of figuring out our plays almost before they got started," Nagurski said. "He was a wonder at backing up the line, a deadly tackler and a tough guy to block out of any play."

Rebholz, a native of Portage, Wisconsin, also lettered for the Wisconsin hockey team in 1928. The Badgers' football MVP in 1929, he was named honorable mention All-America by several organizations. He later spent 36 years as a high school and collegiate coach and administrator.

CHAPTER THREE

The 1930s

T he Great Depression of this era was something of a depression in the fortunes of Badger football, as well. Wisconsin never finished higher than third in the Big Ten in the 1930s, but did feature several outstanding individual performers like Walter F. "Mickey" McGuire and Howard Weiss. Harry Stuhldreher, one of Notre Dame's famed Four Horsemen, took over as head coach in 1936.

McGuire Was MVP in 1932

The multifaceted Walter F. "Mickey" McGuire never earned All-America or first-team All-Big Ten honors during his three-year (1930-1932) career at Wisconsin, but the product of Honolulu, Hawaii, was one of the most electrifying and popular Badgers of his time.

Two of his performances during the 1932 season stand out the most. The first came in the season-opener against Marquette. Midway through the second quarter, one of McGuire's punts was blocked deep in Wisconsin territory. The ball bounced into the end zone and only McGuire's speed allowed him to race back, fall on the ball, and take a safety rather than allow a Marquette touchdown. The Badgers eventually scored a touchdown to take a 7-2 lead, but they needed McGuire's heroics once more.

In the closing seconds of the game, Marquette's Gene Ronzani completed a pass to Dick Quirk, who raced toward the Wisconsin end zone. The swift McGuire caught Quirk, tackled him five yards from the goal line and preserved the Badger victory as time ran out.

Later that season against Minnesota came McGuire's signature performance as a Badger. He had already returned the opening kickoff 90 yards for a touchdown and made a leaping touchdown catch later in the first half. Minnesota, however, tied the game at

The electrifying Mickey McGuire *Photo courtesy of UW Athletic Communications*

13-13 in the third quarter, opening the door for more of McGuire's magic.

Approximately two minutes remained to play when the Badgers took possession of the ball on downs at Minnesota's 43-yard line. Wisconsin proceeded to complete three straight passes. The last one was caught by McGuire who, according to the *Wisconsin State Journal*, "took the ball away from a Minnesota defenseman and fought his way the remaining three yards for a touchdown with Gophers hanging onto his legs and riding his back."

McGuire went on to become managing director of the Hula Bowl for 30 years. He also was president and director of Honolulu Stadium and was managing director of the 1979 Pro Bowl game.

A Legend's Last Game

The legendary Amos Alonzo Stagg has the second most coaching victories in Big Ten games (199) in conference history. His final league game as head coach at the University of Chicago, however, was a loss to the Badgers.

The two schools met in Chicago in the final game of the 1932 season. The Badgers scored one touchdown in each of the game's first three quarters and ended up with an 18-7 victory. Wisconsin's "W" Club gave Stagg an official Wisconsin letter and club membership.

The Badgers finished the 1932 season with a 6-1-1 overall record and their best conference record (4-1-1) in 12 years.

First Victory Over a Ranked Opponent

Wisconsin had played against nationally ranked (by the Associated Press) opponents four times prior to its November 5, 1938, matchup at Northwestern and had lost all four. Now the Badgers had another chance, this time in Evanston against the No. 7 Wildcats.

The Badgers, 3-2 overall, had snapped a two-game losing streak with a 6-0 Homecoming victory over Indiana the weekend before and needed a victory at Northwestern to remain in contention for a Big Ten title. The Wildcats, on the other hand, were not only undefeated at 5-0, but had not allowed a touchdown.

The teams played a scoreless first half before the Badgers finally broke through on standout fullback Howard Weiss's 41-yard touchdown run early in the second half. That gave Wisconsin a lead it never relinquished, and the Badgers went on to a 20-13 victory that featured a 222-85 UW advantage in rushing yardage.

A rabid crowd of fans, estimated by local newspapers at 8,000 strong, greeted the Badgers upon their return to Madison that evening. Wisconsin coach Harry Stuhldreher even addressed the throng briefly from atop a taxi cab.

The victory set up a Big Ten championship match in Madison against Minnesota on November 19, with the winner of that game guaranteed no worse than a share of the league crown.

California, Here We Come

Wisconsin's first football trip to the West Coast was a 2,300-mile train ride that took the Badgers to Los Angeles for a non-conference matchup with UCLA on Saturday, November 12, 1938.

Wisconsin, coached by Harry Stuhldreher (one of Notre Dame's famed Four Horsemen), left three days before the game with 35 players. The Badgers were 4-2 at the time and were coming off a stirring 20-13 upset win at seventh-ranked Northwestern the weekend before.

The Badgers were led by star fullback Howard Weiss, about whom UCLA coach Bill Spaulding said, "If I hadn't seen Bronko Nagurski play, I'd rate Weiss the greatest fullback of them all. The guy is brutal." Weiss went on to finish sixth in the 1938 Heisman Trophy balloting and was a second-round choice of Detroit in the 1939 NFL Draft.

Newspaper accounts of the time made quite an issue of the fact that John Getchell would serve as the field judge for the game between the Badgers and Bruins. Getchell had officiated the Notre Dame-Carnegie Tech game in October of that year. Early in the fourth quarter, as Carnegie Tech was preparing to run a play with the scored tied 0-0, the Tartans' quarterback asked Getchell what down it was. Getchell mistakenly said it was third down when it actually was fourth down. The Fighting Irish ended up taking over and scored three plays later for a 6-0 victory.

Sportswriters referred to Getchell in print as John (What down is it?) Getchell and John (Wrong Down) Getchell.

Getchell was not, however, a factor in this game. Rather, Weiss and Claude York provided the Badgers with one touchdown run apiece, and Wisconsin held on for a 14-7 victory at the Coliseum. The win set up a season-ending showdown with Minnesota the following week.

CHAPTER FOUR

The 1940s

H ead coach Harry Stuhldreher led the Badgers to a pair of second-place finishes in the Big Ten in the Forties, but the 1942 Wisconsin club is one fans of the game will always remember. That team's most notable players (Elroy "Crazylegs" Hirsch, Dave Schreiner, and Pat Harder to name a few) and its signature victory (a 17-7 win over top-ranked Ohio State) are permanently etched in Badger lore. World War II claimed the lives of many college football players, including Schreiner. By the end of the decade, the Badgers had a new coach: Ivy Williamson.

The Horseman

One of the best and most storied teams in Wisconsin history was the 1942 club that finished 8-1-1, was ranked third in the nation, and counted among its victories a 17-7 upset decision over top-ranked Ohio State.

The 1942 squad was loaded with Badger legends like Elroy "Crazylegs" Hirsch, Pat Harder, Mark Hoskins, and Dave Schreiner. It was appropriate, too, that Hirsch, Harder, and Hoskins formed a

Elroy "Crazylegs" Hirsch *Photo courtesy of UW Athletic Communications*

backfield with a nickname (the "Three Hs") because their coach had also played in a backfield with a famous moniker.

Head coach Harry Stuhldreher was the quarterback in the famous Notre Dame backfield that was nicknamed the "Four Horsemen" by Grantland Rice, a sportswriter for the *New York Herald-Tribune*, in 1924. Stuhldreher, along with left halfback Jim Crowley, right halfback Don Miller and fullback Elmer Layden, formed a unit that played 30 career games together and lost to just one team, Nebraska, on two occasions.

Stuhldreher, who ran for 10 touchdowns and passed for 10 more for the Fighting Irish from 1922-1924, coached the Badgers for 13 seasons (1936-1948) and compiled a 45-62-6 record. He also served as the school's athletic director.

The "Crazylegs" Nickname Is Born

One of the most beloved figures in Wisconsin athletic history is the late Elroy "Crazylegs" Hirsch, who starred for the Badgers' powerhouse 1942 team, enjoyed a pro career with the Los Angeles Rams that later landed him in the National Football League Hall of Fame, and served as the UW's director of athletics from 1969-1987.

Hirsch, a native of Wausau, Wisconsin, got his nickname from *Chicago Daily News* sportswriter Francis Powers. As Hirsch was running for a 61-yard touchdown against Great Lakes in 1942, Powers wrote that, "his crazy legs were gyrating in six different directions all at the same time."

The moniker stuck, and the legend was officially born.

A True Hero

The Wisconsin football program has retired four uniform numbers: Elroy "Crazylegs" Hirsch's number 40, Alan "The Horse" Ameche's number 35, Allan Shafer's number 83, and the number 80 that was worn by David Nathan Schreiner.

Hirsch was, of course, a legendary figure in football, starring for the Badgers in 1942 and later serving as the school's athletic director. Ameche was the school's first Heisman Trophy winner. Shafer was the first Badger to die from a football-related injury (during the 1944 game with Iowa). Schreiner's story, however, is particularly unique and poignant.

A native of Lancaster, Wisconsin, Schreiner starred at Wisconsin with lifelong friend and fellow Lancaster product Mark Hoskins, along with standouts like Hirsch and Pat Harder. Those players were key elements on the Badgers' great 1942 team that put together an 8-1-1 record and defeated top-ranked Ohio State.

All-America end Dave Schreiner was killed in action during World War II.
Photo courtesy of UW Athletic Communications

Schreiner, an end who caught three touchdown passes in the second quarter of a 1942 victory over Marquette, was an All-Big Ten and All-America choice in both 1941 and 1942. He was the Big Ten MVP in 1942 and was a second-round draft choice of the Detroit Lions following that campaign.

Like many others of his generation, however, Schreiner, a premedical student, enlisted in the Marine Corps to fight in World War II. He was killed in action on Okinawa on June 21, 1945. He was 24 years old.

Schreiner was the first Wisconsin player elected to the National Football Foundation Hall of Fame. He is also a member of the Wisconsin State Athletic Hall of Fame and the University of Wisconsin Athletic Hall of Fame.

1942 Badgers Topple No. 1 Ohio State

The 1942 Homecoming matchup between the sixth-ranked Badgers and top-ranked Ohio State at Camp Randall Stadium had the pregame hype and buildup worthy of what was called "the nation's outstanding college game" that day.

Massillon, Ohio, products Harry Stuhldreher (Wisconsin) and Paul Brown (Ohio State) would be the coaches matching wits. Stuhldreher was one of the famous Four Horsemen of Notre Dame, while Brown went on to become a football coaching legend. NBC's famed Bill Stern called the game on the radio, with 184 stations carrying it around the nation. A short-wave broadcast brought the game to South America, England, Ireland, Iceland, Hawaii, and Alaska. In addition, both teams were unbeaten.

The Badgers grabbed a 10-0 lead on a touchdown run and field goal by Pat Harder. Ohio State responded with a 17-play, 96-yard touchdown drive that cut the UW lead to 10-7, but the Badgers immediately countered with a 66-yard drive that ended when Elroy "Crazylegs" Hirsch hit Dave Schreiner with a 14-yard scoring strike.

"What I liked best about the game was the way the boys came back to score after Ohio State had ground out 96 yards for its touchdown," Stuhldreher told the *Wisconsin State Journal* after the game.

Hirsch rushed for 118 yards on just 13 carries (a 9.1-yard average) and completed three passes. Harder carried 21 times for 97 yards.

Wisconsin, which moved up to No. 2 in the national rankings after the win, dropped its only game of the season the following week at Iowa by a 6-0 score.

Bucky Is Born

The path to the creation of one of the most popular mascots in college athletics, Bucky Badger, has taken numerous twists and turns over the years.

The early years of Wisconsin football featured live badgers as mascots, but the animals proved too hard to control. The *Badger Yearbook*, in an attempt to maintain a live mascot, even put forth a raccoon named Regdab (badger spelled backward).

Bucky, outfitted in his cardinal and red letter sweater, was drawn first by artist Art Evans in 1940. In those days the Badger mascot had been referred to as Benny, Buddy, Bernie, Bobby and Bouncey.

In 1949, Connie Conrad, a UW-Madison art student, created a papier-mache badger head. Bill Sagal, a gymnast and cheerleader, wore the outfit at the Homecoming game against Iowa and a contest was staged to find a name for the mascot. Buckingham U. Badger, or Bucky, was the winner.

CHAPTER FIVE

The 1950s

Head coaches Ivy Williamson (1949-1956) and Milt Bruhn (1956-1966) guided Wisconsin to one of its most successful decades during the Fifties. Each coach directed the Badgers to a Big Ten title (Williamson in 1952 and Bruhn in 1959), and Wisconsin had its first Heisman Trophy winner when Kenosha, Wisconsin, native Alan "The Horse" Ameche won the coveted award in 1954. The Badgers also finished second in the conference four times during the decade.

Badgers Best Indiana
in Snowy Homecoming Game

It would seem to be difficult to fumble the ball 10 times, lose five of them and still win a football game. That is, however, what the Badgers did in their 6-0 victory over Indiana in the 1951 Homecoming game.

The temperature in Camp Randall Stadium at gametime was just 20 degrees, and a 25-mile-an-hour wind helped blow around snow that tapered off but eventually covered the field.

Wisconsin dominated the game statistically. The Badgers held an 18-5 edge in first downs, a 267-91 advantage in rushing yardage and a 64-0 margin in passing yardage. Ironically, Indiana's only lost fumble of the game gave the Badgers the chance they needed for the win.

Wisconsin recovered halfback Jerry Ellis's fumble at the Indiana 36-yard line with 1:13 remaining to play and the game a scoreless tie. Moments later quarterback John Coatta hit halfback Bill Hutchinson with a 36-yard touchdown pass that gave the Badgers the only points they needed with 58 seconds left.

"I suppose you would call that [the winning pass play] a shot in the dark," Wisconsin head coach Ivy Williamson told the *Wisconsin State Journal* after the game.

The Hard Rocks

One of the ironies of Wisconsin's 1951 football season was that the Badgers owned the nation's No. 1 total defense (154.8 yards per game), the nation's No. 2 run defense (66.8 yards per game), and allowed a mere 5.9 points per game, but had no championship to show for their efforts.

The Badgers started the season with a 22-6 win over intrastate rival Marquette, but lost the following week, 14-10 at eighth-ranked Illinois. The following week came a 6-6 tie at home with Ohio State that left Wisconsin with a 1-1-1 record and, as it turned out, out of contention for the league championship.

That did not, however, diminish a remarkable run of performances by the team's defense the rest of the season. Wisconsin surrendered just 33 points combined in its final seven games, including back-to-back shutout wins over Northwestern and Indiana. None of those last seven opponents scored more than seven points against the Badgers.

The "Hard Rocks," as the 1951 Wisconsin defense was called, actually outscored the Badgers' opponents 58-53 for the season. The school's athletic department even received a letter from a fan who wanted the Badgers to punt on first down so he could watch more of the Wisconsin defense!

Eight of the nine seniors on that defense scored during their careers. Following the season, the defense and the offense played each other in a charity game, with one odd rule: the offense would keep the ball all the time, because the defense felt it could outscore its foes even without the ball.

"Pop" Makes History

Twenty-three Wisconsin football players were named first-team All-Americans from 1912-78, but only one—Ed Withers—was an African-American. Withers's honor came just three years after Jackie Robinson became the first African-American to play Major League Baseball.

Withers was born in Memphis, Tennessee, but was raised in Madison and attended Central High School, where he starred in basketball, football and track. He was, in fact, an All-City selection as a fullback and as a basketball center. Withers, however, joined the Army before finishing high school and spent almost two years with a division of engineers, including a year in Korea.

Withers, nicknamed "Pop," returned to Central, earned his diploma and entered the University of Wisconsin in 1947. He lettered as a defensive back for the Badgers from 1949-1951, picking off eight passes during his career.

The 1950 season was Withers's best. *Look* magazine tabbed him a first-team All-American, and he intercepted three passes for a total of 103 yards in a 14-0 win over Iowa. Harry Grayson of the Newspaper Enterprise Association wrote that Withers was "such a fashionable ball-hawk that just about the only time he got the body contact he likes is when he was tackled after intercepting."

Withers, who was married with a son (Ed III) at the time, went on to earn first-team All-Big Ten and All-America honors as a member of the "Hard Rocks" defense in 1951. He earned a degree in physical education in 1952 and was a draft choice of the Green

Ed Withers starred as a member of the "Hard Rocks" defense in 1951.
Photo courtesy of UW Athletic Communications

Bay Packers. Withers later was a teacher and coach at Milwaukee's Roosevelt and North Division High Schools.

Withers died in 1975 at the age of 48. Upon his death, the Madison NAACP, in a letter to *The Capital Times*, wrote: "We sincerely encourage the Madison Sports Hall of Fame and the Madison Common Council to honor the passing of a great athlete and black man who did much to enable greater black athletic participation."

Recruiting Ameche

Bobby Hinds, a high school football teammate of Alan "The Horse" Ameche, once recounted a story to *The Capital Times* about the recruitment of the back who went on to win the 1954 Heisman Trophy.

Hinds said that Fighting Irish head coach Frank Leahy, a parish priest and Fred Miller, president of Miller Brewing Co., visited Ameche's house to talk to him about attending Notre Dame. Ameche was angered, said Hinds, when Miller produced a $1,500 check and insinuated to Ameche's mother that the check would be hers if her son played for the Irish.

Some Wisconsin fans suggested boycotting Miller beer if Ameche ended up at Notre Dame.

Hinds told *The Capital Times* that Ameche came to Wisconsin in part because he really liked the boxing coaches. Coach Vern Woodward, in fact, gave Ameche and Hinds a ride back to Kenosha, Wisconsin, after finding out the pair had hitchhiked from Kenosha to Madison.

Wisconsin's First Heisman

Modern-day Heisman Trophy presentations are truly tension-filled affairs. The finalists sit in anticipation for almost an hour as television commentators conduct interviews with the players, their families, and their coaches. It builds to "the moment we've all been

Alan "The Horse" Ameche won the 1954 Heisman Trophy.
Photo courtesy of UW Athletic Communications

waiting for," much like the Academy Award-winning movie is traditionally announced at the end of that program.

It does, however, make for good television. Those present at the ceremony, as well as the viewing audience at home, all find out together who has won. But that is not the way it was always done.

The announcement of the 1954 Heisman Trophy winner, Wisconsin's Alan Ameche, came on November 30, but "The Horse" had to wait until December 9 to pick up his hardware. That was the date of the presentation at the Downtown Athletic Club in New York City.

Fans back in Madison could follow the presentation at 9:30 p.m. on WISC Radio. It was televised on New York's WOR-TV.

Incidentally, Ameche won the award with 1,068 points. Kurt Burris, Oklahoma's All-America center, was second with 838 points and Ohio State halfback Howard Cassady was third with 810 points.

The Horse's Favorites

In September of 1954, *Scholastic Magazines*, a publication read by high school students and teachers, was working on a series of stories about several of the nation's top college football players. Badger fullback Alan Ameche was one of the magazine's subjects.

The publication's sports editor put in a request through UW sports publicity director Art Lentz to have Ameche answer several questions. Here were "The Horse's" answers:

Favorite Actor: Gary Cooper
Favorite Actress: Marilyn Monroe
Favorite Singer: Liberace
Favorite Band: University of Wisconsin Band
Favorite School Subject: Anatomy
Hobby: His son, 15-month-old Brian
Ambition: to finish college
Sports Thrill: Being able to play football at Wisconsin and in the Big Ten

Why They Called Him "The Horse"

The derivation of an athlete's nickname can sometimes be unclear, but Heisman Trophy-winning fullback Alan "The Horse" Ameche apparently earned his moniker early in his career at Wisconsin.

According to biographical information compiled by the University of Wisconsin's *Sports News Service*, Ameche was tagged with his nickname during his freshman year in 1951 when sideline observers at a practice watched him "bolt through the tough varsity line, high-stepping and sun-fishing like a mean rodeo bronk."

The name stuck. In fact, when he was introduced as "The Horse" at a pep rally and asked what he would do in the upcoming game, Ameche replied, "I haven't had my oats yet!"

High Praise for Ameche

Few teams were able to corral Wisconsin's Alan "The Horse" Ameche during the fullback's brilliant career, but one team that did was UCLA.

In 1952 the eighth-ranked Bruins knocked off the 10th-ranked Badgers in Madison, 20-7. The following year, UCLA, ranked sixth, won a 13-0 decision over the Badgers in Los Angeles. Ameche gained a total of 81 yards on 27 carries in the two games combined, but that did not stop Bruins coach Red Sanders from heaping praise upon the Badger great.

"[Ameche] is the strongest runner in football history, not even excepting Bronko Nagurski," Sanders said.

Doing the Right Thing

It was 1956, and it had been more than 15 years since the University of Wisconsin track and field team pulled out of a meet at the University of Missouri because local laws prohibited Badger hurdler Ed Smith from participating due to the color of his skin.

Racial segregation, however, was about to affect Badger athletics again.

Men like Ed Withers, Sidney Williams, Cal Vernon, and Robert Teague—early African-American Badger football players—had been performing at Wisconsin since the mid-1940s, so the University took notice when integrated sporting events were banned by law in Louisiana in 1956. The Badgers had already scheduled a home-and-home series with LSU for the 1957 and 1958 seasons.

UW Director of Athletics Ivan Williamson responded to the new law by announcing that the Badgers would not honor their football contract with the Tigers. A statement issued by the UW Department of Athletics said, in part, that, "We have always entered into a contract for athletic contests with another institution on the basis that each school would have complete freedom to select its team members in accordance with the rules and policies of the institution and of the conference of which it is a member. We would be compelled to view any action that interfered with this traditional basic policy of freedom of selection as tantamount to forcing a termination of the contract."

The Louisiana law was thrown out by a federal judge in 1958, a decision later upheld by the United States Supreme Court. The Badgers eventually played at LSU in 1972.

Big Dog

Wisconsin and UNLV would not seem, on the surface, to be two schools that would consistently meet on the football field. But they have and will continue to do so, largely because of the efforts of one man: Tom Wiesner.

"He was a close friend of the program," Wisconsin head coach Barry Alvarez said in 2002. "He was so loyal to our state and the football program and the university. He would come to all our key functions and all the big games. He was always right in the middle of the party."

A native of Neenah, Wisconsin, Wiesner, known as "Big Dog," was a fullback and captain for the Badgers. He scored Wisconsin's only touchdown in the 1960 Rose Bowl. He was a 1961 draft choice of the Baltimore Colts but never played in the NFL. Rather, Wiesner moved to Las Vegas with his wife and went on to become one of the most well-known figures in that city.

Wiesner was a politician and a successful businessman. He also was an avid supporter of his alma mater, as well as UNLV, his adopted hometown school. Wiesner started the Badger Desert Golf Classic during the 1990s, and the event became a big fundraiser for Wisconsin. He also was on the UNLV Board of Regents. In addition, he was instrumental in arranging football games between Wisconsin and UNLV. The two schools played seven times between 1985 and 2004.

Wiesner died of leukemia in 2002. That fall UNLV presented the first Tom Wiesner Award, which is now annually given to a Rebel player who epitomizes the character and toughness displayed by Wiesner as he battled his illness.

1959 Title Earned the Hard Way

They ended up on the wrong end of the most one-sided decision in Wisconsin bowl history, but the 1959 Badgers kept fans on the edge of their seats as they battled their way to the school's first undisputed Big Ten title since 1912.

Led by the versatile Dale Hackbart, who finished seventh in the 1959 Heisman Trophy voting, coach Milt Bruhn's squad was nationally ranked for all but one week of the campaign on its way to a 7-2 regular-season record.

Aside from a 44-6 rout of Marquette, the Badgers won their other six games by an average of just 6.3 points per game. UW's tough defense allowed only 14.9 points per game, but its offense scored just 16.5 points per contest.

Among the Badgers' victories that season were a 12-3 decision at home over coach Woody Hayes's Ohio State team (Wisconsin's only victory over a Hayes-coached Buckeye squad); a 19-10 win at Michigan the following week; and a 24-19 triumph at second-ranked Northwestern, coached by the legendary Ara Parseghian.

The season's crowning achievement, however, came on November 21 against Minnesota in Minneapolis. Wisconsin had lost at home to unranked Illinois by a 9-6 score the week before and needed a victory over the Golden Gophers to lock up at least a share of the conference title.

Things did not start well for Wisconsin. Minnesota won the coin toss, elected to receive, took Jim Bakken's opening kickoff and connected on a 57-yard touchdown pass just four plays into the game. The Golden Gophers had piled up 81 yards in total offense on their first drive. They went on, however, to register just 254 yards the rest of the game.

While the Wisconsin defense was shutting down Minnesota, the Badger offense struggled to score until Karl Holzwarth's then-NCAA record-tying seventh field goal of the season cut the Minnesota lead to 7-3 with 2:16 remaining to play in the third quarter.

The next time the Badgers got the ball, Hackbart, who threw or ran for 223 of Wisconsin's 321 yards in the game, drove his team 80 yards for the game-winning touchdown. Appropriately, it was Hackbart who scored the touchdown and passed to Henry Derleth for an important two-point conversion. For good measure, Hackbart intercepted a Minnesota pass on the game's final play.

The Badgers fell 44-8 to Washington in the Rose Bowl on New Year's Day of 1960. But the team's place in school history is secure as one of just three (1962 and 1999 are the others) Wisconsin squads since 1912 to win an undisputed Big Ten championship.

CHAPTER SIX

The 1960s

The decade started well for the Badgers as head coach Milt Bruhn guided Wisconsin to a 14-5 overall record in 1961-1962, including a Big Ten championship in 1962 and an appearance in one of the most famous bowl games of all time: the 1963 Rose Bowl. Following that season, however, the program began a downward spiral amid the social unrest of the era, and ended the decade with a 3-26-1 record under head coach John Coatta from 1967-1969.

The Badgers and The Warriors

The annual Wisconsin-Marquette men's basketball game has long been a contest fans from both schools point to for state bragging rights. The Badgers and Warriors (as they were formerly known), however, also played 36 intercollegiate football games between 1904 and 1960.

The Badgers were 32-4 in the all-time series with their rivals to the east and won the last 17 meetings.

The final game between Wisconsin and Marquette was played at Camp Randall Stadium on October 1, 1960. The Badgers used two field goals from Jim Bakken and a pair of pass interception returns for touchdowns to key a 35-6 victory.

Incidentally, Marquette's sports publicity director at the time was Bob Harlan, who later became president and chief executive officer of the Green Bay Packers.

The Famous First Date

How did a broken collar bone result in a successful marriage that has lasted more than 40 years? Here's the story.

The year was 1960 and sophomore end Pat Richter had told teammate Brad Armstrong that Armstrong's girlfriend, Barb, knew someone Richter was interested in meeting and asked if Barb would tell her friend that Richter might see her at a State Street drugstore called Rennebohm's.

Richter showed up at Rennebohm's that night, spotted Milwaukee native Renee Sengstock and introduced himself. Richter did not get the response he had hoped for. Sengstock had not heard from Armstrong's girlfriend and, therefore, had no idea who Richter was.

"She had a 'who are you?' look on her face," Richter recalled. "But we talked a bit, I ended up dropping her off at the library a couple times and we decided to go out on a date after the Michigan game [on October 29]."

Richter was enjoying a solid season, but went down funny on his shoulder after his first reception against the Wolverines and knew immediately that he had broken his collar bone. "I could feel the bone in my shoulder," he said. "I walked right down in front of the bench, told the coaches I broke my collar bone and just kept walking toward the tunnel."

Sengstock, meanwhile, was discovering that her seat at Camp Randall Stadium was right next to another young lady who claimed to have a date that night with Richter. "I apparently had given Renee a ticket, and this other gal had one and they were sitting there

Pat Richter (88) was an All-America end and later served as Director of Athletics at Wisconsin. *Photo courtesy of UW Athletic Communications*

talking and figured out that they both had a date with me," Richter said.

Sengstock, however, kept the date. She showed up at the hospital to visit Richter that evening, while the other young woman did not. "As Renee tells it, they were going over my medical history and said I was Lutheran," Richter said. "Renee said her eyes lit up, because she hadn't met many Lutheran boys."

The pair eventually had their first "real" date soon after when they went to see *Ben Hur*. They got engaged a couple years later and were married in June of 1963.

They Remember the Comeback

In some ways it was the equivalent of what we now know to be the Bowl Championship Series national title game. It was No. 1 vs.

Milt Bruhn coached the Badgers to Big Ten titles in 1959 and 1962.
Photo courtesy of UW Athletic Communications

No. 2. It was Southern California against Wisconsin in the 1963 Rose Bowl.

The Trojans took leads of 28-7 and 42-14 before the Badgers, led by quarterback Ron Vander Kelen and end Pat Richter, rallied for 23 unanswered, fourth-quarter points. USC won, 42-37, but most seem to recall "the comeback" rather than the final score.

"People seem to remember that game as entertainment," says Richter. "They don't say 'remember that game you lost?' They say, 'remember that Rose Bowl, what a great game.' You really recognized that the game had an entertainment value to it rather than who won or lost."

That point was driven home to Richter more than 30 years later. While he and coach Barry Alvarez were in Pasadena for a meeting in the weeks leading up to the Badgers' 1994 Rose Bowl appearance, the two ran into former Los Angeles Dodgers manager Tommy Lasorda.

"Barry introduced himself," Richter recalls. "Lasorda said, 'Hey, Coach, how are you doing?' I said, 'Pat Richter.' All of a sudden Lasorda is saying, 'Boy that was a great game, that Rose Bowl' and so on. Barry must have been thinking, 'What is going on here?'"

A Sign of Things to Come

Wisconsin's highest-scoring game of the modern era wound up serving notice that Badger fans might be in for something special in 1962.

The unranked Badgers, coming off a 1961 campaign during which they went 6-3 after finishing with three straight victories, opened the 1962 campaign by hosting New Mexico State at Camp Randall Stadium on September 29. The Aggies never had a chance.

Wisconsin's Jim Nettles scored his team's first touchdown of the season when he picked off a James Head pass and took it 89 yards for the third-longest interception return in school history with 9:04 left in the first quarter. The floodgates had opened as seven different Badgers scored en route to a 69-6 lead after three quarters.

The Badgers won, 69-13, and in the process put up more points than any Wisconsin club had since an 85-0 victory over Marquette in 1915. UW proceeded to average 32.2 points per game that season, a modern-era school record at the time that stood until 1983. The Badgers finished the season with a 42-37 loss to Southern California in the thrilling 1963 Rose Bowl game.

No. 1 No More

Maybe it was the karma provided by members of the 1912 Wisconsin football team. Maybe it was the challenge of playing the top-ranked team in the country. Or maybe the Badgers had simply started to smell the roses.

Whatever forces were at work, they worked. The Badgers have defeated the No. 1-ranked team in the nation three times in school history, but their 37-6 rout of Northwestern on November 10, 1962, was as impressive a win (especially given the circumstances) as the school has had.

A Camp Randall Stadium-record crowd of 65,501, including a dozen players from the Badgers' undefeated 1912 Big Ten championship squad (which defeated Northwestern 56-0 that season), showed up to see if Wisconsin could win its Homecoming game for the first time since 1958.

"We'd had a nice start to the season, but I don't know if we really knew how good we could be," All-America end Pat Richter recalled later. "Maybe they [Northwestern] had a bad day and we had a good day, but we really took them apart."

The Wildcats, under head coach Ara Parseghian, brought a 6-0 record into the game but never got anything going offensively. Northwestern punted three times and turned the ball over on downs near the end of the first half, while Wisconsin was taking a 10-0 lead at the break.

UW then broke the game open. Back Gary Kroner scored his second touchdown of the afternoon on a 23-yard pass from quarterback Ron Vander Kelen, and Lou Holland tallied three second-half touchdowns (two rushing and one receiving).

The Badgers had improved to 6-1 with just two conference games left, but head coach Milt Bruhn would listen to no Rose Bowl talk. Instead, he borrowed a time-honored sporting cliché when reporters queried him after the win about Pasadena: "We think about just one game at a time."

November 22, 1963

It was abnormal for Wisconsin to be playing a regular-season football game on Thanksgiving. The Thanksgiving holiday in 1963, however, was anything but normal.

The Badgers had started the 1963 campaign with four straight victories, but had lost three of their next four, slipping to 5-3 as they headed into the season finale at Minnesota on November 23. The Golden Gophers were just 2-6 and were looking to finish with a win over their rivals to the east.

Wisconsin left Madison for Minneapolis via United Airlines charter at 2:00 p.m. on Friday, November 22, but they had more on their minds than a football game. They had, in fact, just received the news that President John F. Kennedy had been assassinated in Dallas.

Talk of postponing the game had already started by the time the Badgers checked into the Curtis Hotel, and official word came just after 8:00 p.m. In fact, all Big Ten games were postponed that day, including the Illinois-Michigan State game in East Lansing that was to decide the league title and Big Ten Rose Bowl representative.

The Badgers and Golden Gophers kicked off at 10:30 a.m. on Thanksgiving Day (November 28), and Minnesota proceeded to win the 73rd meeting between the two schools, 14-0.

The All-Time Team

College football celebrated its centennial in 1969, and Badger fans were asked to select an all-time Wisconsin team. Eleven players were chosen, with 1954 Heisman Trophy winner Alan Ameche honored as the "All-time Greatest Player."

The remaining players included: Ken Bowman (1961-63), Howard "Cub" Buck (1913-15), Pat Harder (1941-42), Elroy "Crazylegs" Hirsch (1942), Dan Lanphear (1957-59), Arlie Mucks Sr. (1914), Pat Richter (1960-62), Dave Schreiner (1940-42), Ron Vander Kelen (1962), and Robert "Red" Wilson (1946-49).

Twenty-Three

Wisconsin and Iowa played 80 football games against each other between 1894 and 2004. The Badgers won 39 times, as did the Hawkeyes, and there were two ties. But few, if any, of the Wisconsin wins were celebrated with the enthusiasm and sense of relief that Badger players and their fans felt after UW's 23-17 victory at Camp Randall Stadium on October 11, 1969.

A little bit of background is necessary to understand why that win kicked off such a wild celebration.

First, Wisconsin had not won a football game since a 7-6 victory at home over Minnesota on November 19, 1966. The Badgers were winless in 23 consecutive games and had lost 18 in a row. In addition, the UW-Madison campus had developed a well-earned reputation as a hotbed of anti-Vietnam War protest. The social and political unrest of that era had an effect on the entire campus. Finally, the Badgers had endured a number of frustrating close calls during the skid, including a 21-20 loss to Indiana on Homecoming in 1968. Wisconsin missed five field goal attempts that day.

It was against this backdrop that the Badgers took the field to play host to Iowa. Things did not, however, start well for Wisconsin. In fact, head coach John Coatta's Badgers fell behind 17-0 before fullback Alan "A-Train" Thompson scored a pair of fourth-quarter touchdowns (the second one with 4:50 remaining) to cut the Iowa lead to 17-14.

Wisconsin forced the Hawkeyes to punt on their next possession and, moments later (with 2:08 left), quarterback Neil

Graff hit junior receiver Randy Marks with a 17-yard touchdown pass on fourth down-and-11. Roger Jaeger's conversion gave the Badgers a 21-17 advantage.

Iowa's Dennis Green fumbled the ensuing kickoff and ended up downing the ball in the endzone for a Wisconsin safety. Jaeger missed a field goal attempt on the Badgers' next possession, but Neovia Greyer's interception ended Iowa's final possession and touched off a massive celebration.

Thousands from the crowd of 53,714 followed the Wisconsin Band right out of Camp Randall Stadium and paraded through the streets of campus and downtown Madison. "When we finally won, it was crazy," UW Band director Mike Leckrone, who was in his first year at Wisconsin, recalled later. "Even in the Rose Bowls, I've never seen the fans so giddy."

Wisconsin's 23-game winless streak ended thanks to a 23-point fourth-quarter, during which the game-winning touchdown was scored by Marks, who, of course, wore number 23.

"Grape Juice"

Wisconsin entered the 1969 season in the throes of the worst period of futility in its football history. Head coach John Coatta's Badgers were 0-19-1 over the previous two seasons. They did, however, have a bright, young star halfback upon which to pin their hopes: Greg "Grape Juice" Johnson.

Sophomore running backs like Ralph Kurek, Alan "The Horse" Ameche and Elroy "Crazylegs" Hirsch had duly impressed prior generations of Badger fans. Now it would be Johnson's turn. The East St. Louis, Illinois, native was even projected by some to be the Heisman Trophy winner as a senior in 1971!

Johnson once explained the derivation of his nickname. "My mother always called me 'Grape,' except when she was mad at me," he said. "Then she called me Gregory. My teammates added the 'Juice.'"

Johnson even challenged Hirsch by having the Badger legend run some pass patterns on him. The former Los Angeles Rams star beat Johnson three times, prompting the youngster to say, "Man, that cat's got some moves."

There would be no Heisman in Johnson's future. He rushed for 166 yards and one touchdown in eight games in 1969. He never carried the ball in a game again. Johnson, however, did set the school record for career kickoff return yardage with 1,081 in the two seasons (1969 and 1971) in which he played. He still holds the school mark for career kickoff return average (24.6 yards per return).

Johnson also excelled with the Badger track and field team. He set school records for the indoor and outdoor long jump as well as the 60-yard high hurdles. He also won four Big Ten individual titles during this career.

CHAPTER SEVEN

The 1970s

Wisconsin enjoyed just two winning seasons during the decade, but Badger fans saw a number of outstanding players (Rufus "Roadrunner" Ferguson, Bill Marek, Mike Webster and Dennis Lick among them) in this era. Head coach Dave McClain arrived in 1978 and ended up taking the school to three bowl games in eight seasons. The 1970s also marked the debut of what is now known to Wisconsin fans as the Fifth Quarter.

Rufus Visits Madison

Rufus "Roadrunner" Ferguson's energetic personality and bright smile were never more evident than on the day he made his official visit to Wisconsin.

Wisconsin assistant coach LaVern Van Dyke told the *Wisconsin State Journal* that he went to pick up Ferguson at the airport with temperatures below freezing and wind chills making it feel even colder.

Ferguson hopped off the plane, having traveled from Miami, Florida, wearing a white suit and no overcoat. When Van Dyke yelled his name, Ferguson hustled over to him and replied: "How'd ya know it was me?"

Billy Marek, who took over as the program's premier back once Ferguson had left, remembers the "Roadrunner's" upbeat outlook on life.

"He was a guy who would walk into a room and just light it up," Marek said. "He just loved being around people. I remember him and I being among the last ones left in the locker room after a game, and he stood in front of a mirror for about 20 minutes just fixing his hat. You could just see how much he enjoyed every moment he spent with the football program."

The Roadrunner

Wisconsin's great tradition of running backs has produced a pair of Heisman Trophy winners (Alan Ameche and Ron Dayne), as well as others like Terrell Fletcher, Brent Moss, Billy Marek and Anthony Davis.

Few, if any, of those players, however, brought the personality and flamboyance (as well as talent) to Camp Randall Stadium that Rufus "Roadrunner" Ferguson did during his three-year career from 1970-1972.

Ferguson, who got his nickname from his base-stealing exploits as a ballplayer in his hometown of Miami, left Wisconsin as the second-leading rusher in school history behind Ameche. Ferguson, who rushed for 100 yards 11 times during his career, also set the school record for rushing yards in a season when he carried 249 times for 1,222 yards and 13 touchdowns as a junior in 1971.

Ferguson, an Academic All-American in 1972, enjoyed the second most productive rushing game in school history (at that point in time) when he rushed for 211 yards in a 23-21 loss to Minnesota in the final game of the 1971 season.

At the conclusion of his senior year, Ferguson was recognized at a banquet at the Pfister Hotel in Milwaukee. Ferguson described it as "the greatest moment of my life." Then-UW director of athletics

Rufus "Roadrunner" Ferguson thrilled Badger fans during the early 1970s.
Photo courtesy of UW Athletic Communications

Elroy Hirsch thanked Ferguson "for all the excitement and thrills, not to mention all the fannies you put in the seats."

April Fool!

College football players switch positions all the time. A fullback might be turned into a linebacker. An offensive lineman may move to the defensive line. It happens all the time. All-Big Ten running backs, however, usually don't become defensive backs, but that is what Badger fans were led to believe one April morning in 1975.

Billy Marek, the Big Ten rushing leader and nation's leading scorer as a junior in 1974, was set to enter his senior year on track to become Wisconsin's career rushing leader. Marek had rushed for 2,422 yards and 31 touchdowns the two previous seasons combined, including a remarkable 304-yard, five-touchdown performance in the final game of his junior year against Minnesota.

It therefore made no sense to Badger fans who picked up the *Wisconsin State Journal* on April 1 and read a story by reporter Tom Butler that claimed Marek was being moved to free safety because Badger coach John Jardine had an abundance of tailbacks and was looking for a backup for safety Steve Wagner, who had undergone knee surgery in the offseason.

"If it helps the team, I'll gladly move," Butler claimed Marek had said. "I can't do much more than last year anyway. Let somebody else have a chance."

The news had wire service reporters calling Jardine at home for confirmation, and the Associated Press even moved the story on its national wire before later killing it.

What many readers of the newspaper failed to see was the last line of the story that simply said: "April Fool!"

A Swift Kick in the Pants

Billy Marek was just the second Badger ever to rush for 1,000 yards in a season. He set the school record for rushing yards and touchdowns in a game. He was a three-time, first-team All-Big Ten selection. But even Marek was not immune to the need for an occasional wake-up call.

Marek was standing on the sideline during a game one day when he felt the sudden impact of a shoe hitting his backside. It was assistant coach Chuck McBride.

"What are you doing out there?" the coach asked Marek. The running back responded by asking McBride what he was talking about. "You're sleepwalking out there," McBride said. "Wake up!"

Nowadays that type of motivational ploy might result in a lawsuit. Marek, however, appreciated it.

"I thought it was the appropriate move," Marek said. "We all need another viewpoint sometimes. I think sometimes we think we're just fine, but we're really just going through the motions and running in place."

Eight-Year Teammates

It is unusual enough that two players would have played their entire high school and college careers together, but it is extremely rare that three players would have done so. That's why former Badgers running back Billy Marek, offensive tackle Dennis Lick, and center Joe Norwick appreciated it so much.

The trio starred together at St. Rita's High School, a football power on the south side of Chicago that won all 13 of its games and the city championship in 1971. By their junior years, the college recruiting process had begun.

"Our high school coach, Pat Cronin, was very aware of the types of things he felt we should consider during the process—what type of offense a school was running, how many freshmen and sophomores were on the roster, the community as a whole," Marek said. "Wisconsin had been recruiting us since our junior year in high school. Going to Madison, there was virtually no change in the offense from the style we were running in high school. Even our school colors were exactly the same!"

Marek, Lick, and Norwick were together at Wisconsin from 1972-1975 and helped lead the Badgers to the school's only winning season (a 7-4 mark in 1974) from 1964-1977. Marek became a three-time, first-team All-Big Ten selection and the school's career rushing leader. Lick was a consensus All-American and first-round draft choice of the Chicago Bears, and Norwick earned two letters as the successor to center Mike Webster.

Three Games, 740 Yards and 13 Touchdowns

Any list of legendary individual Wisconsin football feats would have to include running back Billy Marek's rushing performance over the final three games of the 1974 season.

The junior from Chicago tied 1973 Heisman Trophy winner John Cappaletti's NCAA record for consecutive 200-yard rushing efforts when he blitzed Iowa, Northwestern, and Minnesota for a total of 740 yards and a remarkable 13 touchdowns. Marek, however, has never considered his achievement to be an individual one.

"The offensive line was tremendous," Marek said. "I can remember in the Iowa game, there were so many holes to run through that it was hard to choose. The O-line was just in its glory."

Marek shredded the Hawkeyes for 206 yards and four touchdowns on 34 carries in a 28-15 victory in Iowa City. He came back the following week to gain 230 yards and three scores in a 52-7 blowout at Northwestern. What could he do for an encore?

Despite running on a wet field and having a 65-yard touchdown run called back because of a clipping penalty, Marek broke the school record for rushing yards (304) and touchdowns (five).

It is difficult to ascertain where the credit for Marek's greatest performance belongs. "There were so many places to run in that Minnesota game that I was actually exhausted by the end," said Marek, heaping praise on his blockers.

Lineman Terry Stieve thought otherwise after the game: "I don't think the offensive line can take credit today. He [Marek] looked like he was doing it all on his own."

Billy Marek set the Wisconsin career record for rushing yards.
Photo courtesy of UW Athletic Communications

Shocking The Cornhuskers

Between 1964 and 1977, the Wisconsin football program had just one (1974) winning season, but that campaign was filled with memorable performances and moments. Perhaps none was as thrilling, however, as quarterback Gregg Bohlig's 77-yard touchdown pass to Jeff Mack that beat fourth-ranked Nebraska at Camp Randall Stadium on September 22.

Wisconsin started the 1974 campaign with a 28-14 victory at Purdue and returned to Madison with Coach Tom Osborne's No. 4-ranked Cornhuskers set to visit for the home opener the following weekend.

The two teams played to a statistical draw by halftime, but Nebraska led 14-7. The Cornhuskers then added a third-quarter field goal for a 17-7 advantage with 10:15 remaining in the period. Late in the third quarter, however, the Badger defense stopped Nebraska on a fourth-and-one try at the Wisconsin 27-yard line. The Badgers took possession and began their march to victory.

Bohlig engineered an eight-play, 73-yard scoring drive that ended when running back Billy Marek crossed the goal line from one yard out with 14:16 remaining to play in the game. The Cornhuskers added another field goal for a 20-14 lead with only 4:21 left on the clock.

The Badgers took over on their own 29-yard line with 4:13 remaining. Bohlig was dropped for a six-yard loss, setting up what would become one of the most memorable second-and-16 conversions in school history.

Bohlig rolled out and hit Mack, who was bumped by a Nebraska defender while the ball was in the air, at the Wisconsin 45-yard line. Mack, whose son, Jeff, went on to start at linebacker for the Badgers, then finished off the 77-yard scoring strike by racing down the sideline for the touchdown.

"It was one of our normal plays," Badger head coach John Jardine said after the game. "Jeff runs an 'out' pattern and if he's covered tightly, he turns upfield. We practice it every day. My only concern about it was that he might go out of bounds."

Mack, of course, did not go out of bounds and, after Vince Lamia's extra point, Wisconsin led 21-20 with 3:29 remaining to play. The Badgers got an interception from Steve Wagner with 2:40 left and ran out the clock after that.

Split end Art Sanger said of Mack after the game: "Jeff Mack just keeps on coming back. We were all trying to get to him after the TD, and that's just about the only place you can catch Jeff Mack—in the end zone."

The First of Three

There have been three 100-yard kickoff returns in modern-era Wisconsin football history. The first was brought back by Ira Matthews against Iowa in 1976. Michael Jones did it against Northwestern in 1984, and Aaron Stecker turned the trick at Minnesota in 1995.

Matthews's return, however, was the first of the three, and came in a game whose meaning increased annually for two decades.

The Badgers were 3-5 overall and 1-4 in Big Ten play when they met head coach Bob Commings's Hawkeyes (4-4 and 2-3) on Homecoming at Camp Randall Stadium on November 6, 1976. Iowa took a 14-13 lead before the Badgers went ahead 23-14 after three quarters. The Hawkeyes narrowed the Wisconsin advantage to 23-21 with just 6:54 remaining to play in the game. Then Matthews made his mark.

The Wisconsin sophomore collected the ensuing kickoff and promptly returned it 100 yards for a touchdown. Iowa eventually fumbled the ball away on its next possession, and Matthews ended up scoring on a 15-yard run with 1:59 left.

"I just saw a lot of bodies to get through," Matthews said afterward of his kickoff return. "I went up the middle and bounced to where the lane was. I just had to read the blocks. Everybody gave me good blocks, and I just ran with it."

No one knew that it would be another 21 years (and two days) before the Badgers would defeat their rivals to the southwest. Commings guided the Hawkeyes to wins over Wisconsin in 1977 and 1978. Hayden Fry took over for Commings in 1979 and coached Iowa to a 15-0-1 record against Wisconsin before the Badgers upset the 12th-ranked Hawkeyes, 13-10, on Homecoming in Madison on November 8, 1997.

The Portage Plumber

Fans of the successful Barry Alvarez era at Wisconsin—a period that included 108 wins and three Big Ten and Rose Bowl titles in its first 15 years—might be surprised to find out that there was a time when football was not necessarily the main attraction at Badger homes games.

Wisconsin enjoyed just two winning seasons from 1964 through 1980. The teams were not winning, but Badger supporters had plenty of individuals to keep them coming back. Running backs like Alan "A-Train" Thompson, Rufus "The Roadrunner" Ferguson, and Billy Marek helped keep things interesting on Saturdays at Camp Randall Stadium. So did the Portage Plumber.

Terry Westegard, a steam-fitter from Portage, Wisconsin, was a highlight all his own at Badger home games from 1976-82. Decked out in a skirt, furry helmet and pom-pons, Westegard would emerge from the stands in the fourth quarter and provide fans with a laugh as he joined the cheerleaders' "kick line."

Wisconsin, however, started the 1981 season by stunning top-ranked Michigan 21-14 at Camp Randall Stadium. The Badgers went on to a 7-5 record that year and an appearance in the Garden State Bowl. Head coach Dave McClain was ushering in a new era at Wisconsin, and it signaled the decline of the Portage Plumber, whose act disappeared following the 1982 campaign.

You've Said It All

Fans who stuck around in Camp Randall Stadium until the end of the Badgers' 22-19 victory over Oregon on September 30, 1978, witnessed one of the great comeback wins in school history. That was obvious.

What may not have been as clear to those in attendance that day were the historic happenings in the stadium that have become as much a part of Badger football lore as Alan Ameche, Ron Dayne, or Lee Evans.

The Wisconsin Band had been performing at home hockey games for several years when, during a game in 1973, fans started clamoring for a polka to be played. The closest thing the band had to a polka was a song that had been used as a beer commercial as well as a country tune (written by Steve Karmen) called "When You Say Love, You've Said It All." Band director Mike Leckrone made a couple adjustments and soon the "You've Said It All," (known to fans as the "Bud Song") was a favorite with fans who finished it by singing in unison, "When you say WIS-CON-SIN, you've said it all!"

The song really took off, however, the day the Badgers scored all their points in the fourth quarter and erased a 19-7 Oregon lead in the final seven minutes of the game. In an effort to "fire up" the Camp Randall Stadium crowd, Leckrone had the band play "You've Said It All." Moments later third-string quarterback Mike Kalasmiki hit David Charles with a 26-yard touchdown pass to cut the Oregon lead to 13-7 with 10:29 remaining to play.

The Ducks responded with a touchdown of their own and led 19-7 with 7:07 left. The band again played "You've Said It All," and the Badgers connected on a 49-yard touchdown pass that was called back due to an interference penalty. But the "Bud Song" also preceded a 12-yard scoring pass from Kalasmiki to Tim Stracka with 2:14 remaining. Wisconsin then recovered an onside kick and won the game when Kevin Cohee scored from four yards out with 1:32 left in the game.

The playing of "You've Said It All" stirred up a great deal of discussion and concern, because when the band played it, the upper deck of Camp Randall Stadium swayed and shook as fans sang and danced along. In addition, there was concern over the appropriateness of using a beer commercial at a university activity. Public opinion, however, won out in favor of the song. As for the edgy Badger supporters, Leckrone eventually began making a tongue-in-cheek announcement the rest of the season that warned nervous fans in advance of the playing of the "Bud Song."

"That game against Oregon really not only gave the 'Bud Song' its takeoff, but it became the basis for the Fifth Quarter," Leckrone said. "We had been staying and playing for the crowd afterward, but it didn't have the kind of raw activity that we've got now. One sort of led to the other."

The "Bud Song" and the Fifth Quarter (the band's on-the-field, postgame show) are now, of course, staples at every Badger home football game.

Two Special Awards

Like most college football programs, Wisconsin hands out a variety of team awards at the conclusion of each season. Individual honors are bestowed upon the most valuable player, scout team players of the year, special teams player of the year, and the team's best scholastic achiever.

Wisconsin, however, has two more awards that carry particular significance. They are the Jay Seiler Coaches Appreciation Award (defense) and the Wayne Souza Coaches Appreciation Award (offense).

Jay Seiler was a 19-year-old freshman defensive back from Schofield, Wisconsin, when he injured himself making a tackle during a spring practice in 1979. He collapsed and became unconscious. Seiler died a week later, on April 7, at Madison General Hospital. Doctors said he had suffered cerebral or brain death.

Just less than four months after Seiler's tragic death, Wayne Souza, who was entering his senior year with the Badgers, drowned after jumping into Madison's Lake Monona for a swim. Souza had lettered twice for the Badgers and had caught 24 passes for 323 yards and three touchdowns as a junior.

"I'm stunned by the drowning of Wayne Souza," Wisconsin head coach Dave McClain said at the time. "I'm in total shock. Wayne Souza was one of the finest young men I've met in athletics."

CHAPTER EIGHT

The 1980s

ead coach Dave McClain (1978-1985) took the Badgers to bowl games in 1981, 1982 and 1984, but his sudden death signaled a decline in the program from 1986-1989 when the Badgers suffered through a cumulative 9-36 record under coaches Jim Hilles (1986) and Don Morton (1987-1989). Individually however, Badgers like Al Toon, Tim Krumrie, and Paul Gruber shone brightly on Saturdays at Camp Randall Stadium.

1981 Started with a Bang

Athletics can be a little bit like the stock market. What has happened in the past is not necessarily an indication of what will happen in the future. Wisconsin validated that statement when it opened the 1981 season with a 21-14 victory over top-ranked Michigan.

The Wolverines definitely had history on their side. Wisconsin had not defeated Michigan since 1962, a string of 14 straight losses. Furthermore, the Badgers had only beaten the Wolverines once in Madison. And to underline Wisconsin's more recent futility against

Michigan, one only had to see that the Wolverines had outscored the Badgers 176-0 in four meetings from 1977-1980.

Wisconsin took a 14-7 halftime lead only to have Michigan's Butch Woolfolk tie the game on an 89-yard touchdown run with 9:17 left to play in the third quarter. The Badgers then started their next possession on their own 19-yard line. Facing third-down-and-nine from the Wisconsin 29, Badger quarterback Jess Cole threw a screen pass to tailback John Williams, who raced 71 yards for what proved to be the game-winning score.

The Badger defense, which had allowed Michigan an average of 44 points per game in the previous four meetings, limited the Wolverines to just 14 points and 229 yards of total offense. Wisconsin was paced by defensive lineman Tim Krumrie's 13 tackles and safety Matt Vanden Boom's three interceptions, all of which came during Michigan's final six possessions.

"Obviously Wisconsin is a better team than everyone thought, and obviously we aren't as good as everyone thought," Michigan head coach Bo Schembechler said after the game. "This isn't 1980."

Good Guess

Head coach Dave McClain may not have predicted the final score of the 1981 Wisconsin-Michigan game, but he clearly visualized success for the Badgers.

Two days before the Badgers were to square off against the No. 1-ranked Wolverines to start the season, McClain had "Wisconsin 17, Michigan 14" illuminated on the scoreboard during practice at Camp Randall Stadium.

Forty-eight hours later McClain had one of the biggest victories of his coaching career, a 21-14 decision over coach Bo Schembechler's mighty Wolverines.

Tim Krumrie: Tenacity, Toughness and Talent

Who better to describe the way former Badger noseguard Tim Krumrie played than someone who played against him?

Tim Krumrie was one of the best defensive players in school history.
Photo courtesy of UW Athletic Communications

"Everything they said about him is true," said Tennessee center Lee North after facing Krumrie in the 1981 Garden State Bowl. "He's the best guy that I've gone against this year. I think he's a great ball player. He's got everything—speed, quickness, strength. He just jumps on you and beats you half to death. I'm very sore right now, very sore."

One of the great defensive players ever to wear a Wisconsin uniform, Krumrie's 444 career tackles are more than any defensive lineman in school history and his 276 solo tackles still rank first in UW annals for any position. He started all 46 games during his career (1979-1982) and was named first-team All-Big Ten three times and first-team All-American twice.

Some of Krumrie's best performances came in big games. He was named the MVP of the 1982 Independence Bowl, a Badger win over Kansas State. He also was named national defensive player of the week by the Associated Press for his role in Wisconsin's 21-14 upset win over top-ranked Michigan in the 1981 season opener.

"If there was a street fight, the guy who never stops is Krumrie," former Wisconsin head coach Dave McClain once told the *Milwaukee Journal.* "You can block him, but you better hang on 'till the whistle blows, because he's never gonna quit."

Krumrie went on to play for the Cincinnati Bengals from 1983-1994. He played in the 1988 and 1989 Pro Bowls.

The Bounce Pass

One of the most notable plays in modern-era Badger football occurred when Wisconsin was hosting Illinois at Camp Randall Stadium in 1982.

The Badgers, riding a four-game winning streak, had fallen behind 26-20 after Illinois's Mike Bass kicked a 44-yard field goal with 4:03 remaining to play in the game. Wisconsin quarterback Randy Wright was intercepted on the next possession, but the Badgers recorded a safety when Illinois punter Chris Sigourney ran into the end zone. UW received Sigourney's free kick, trailing 26-22.

Wright moved the Badgers to the Illinois 40-yard line. On second down and 10, Wright skipped a bounce pass to receiver Al

Toon. Thinking it was an incomplete pass, the Illini defense relaxed. Toon then connected with Jeff Nault, who scored to put Wisconsin ahead 28-26 with just 52 seconds left to play.

"We worked on the double pass this week," Badger head coach Dave McClain said after the game. "It is supposed to bounce just like it did. The bounce makes it look like the play was incomplete. Like any other special play, I inform the officials beforehand so they know what to watch for."

The Badgers, however, missed the extra point, a failure that came back to haunt them moments later when Illinois quarterback Tony Eason engineered a 51-yard drive that lasted 52 seconds and ended with Bass's Big Ten record-tying fifth field goal of the game from 46 yards out as time expired.

The entertaining contest featured 958 yards in combined total offense, including a career-high 479 yards passing by Eason.

A First at Ohio Stadium

Visiting teams have not often found themselves on the winning side of the final score at Ohio State over the years, but when the Badgers traveled to Columbus for an October 9, 1982, matchup with the Buckeyes, they were looking to become the first Wisconsin team ever to win at Ohio Stadium. In fact, Wisconsin's only win at Ohio State was in 1918, but that was four years before Ohio Stadium was built.

Ironically, all the Badgers needed to defeat the Buckeyes that rainy afternoon was the touchdown they scored on their first possession of the game.

Ohio State's Rich Spangler missed a field goal attempt to end the Buckeyes' game-opening drive. Wisconsin took over, drove 80 yards in 14 plays, and tailback John Williams scored from one yard out. Mark Doran's extra-point try was blocked, leaving Wisconsin with a 6-0 lead that stood for the duration of the game.

Ohio State had one last chance early in the fourth quarter when it intercepted a Randy Wright pass. Buckeye tailback Tim Spencer, however, turned the ball back over when he fumbled with 8:33 remaining to play. The Badgers, remarkably, held the ball the rest of the game as Wright guided them on a game-ending, 17-play drive that included two successful fourth-down conversions.

Wisconsin head coach Dave McClain told reporters after the game that it was his "biggest win as a coach."

The Greatest Comeback

There have been plenty of stirring comeback victories in Badger football history. But never before and never since has Wisconsin come back from a larger deficit so late in a game as it did in a shocker at Missouri in 1984.

When Missouri's Brad Burditt kicked a point-after following an 18-yard touchdown reception by George Shorthose, the Tigers led Wisconsin 28-7 with just 4:42 remaining to play in the third quarter. Then Badger cornerback Richard Johnson took over.

Missouri faced fourth down and 12 from its own 18-yard line as Marlon Adler lined up to punt the ball away. Cornerback Bobby Taylor blocked it, and Johnson recovered the ball and scored with 14:56 left in the fourth quarter.

The Tigers then faced fourth down and 17 from their own 12-yard line on their next possession. Johnson partially blocked another Adler punt that gave the Badgers possession on Missouri's 37-yard line. The sixth play of the ensuing Wisconsin drive was a nine-yard touchdown pass from quarterback Mike Howard to receiver Al Toon.

The Tigers failed to score on their next drive, and less than two minutes later Howard hit Toon from 24 yards out. Todd Gregoire's extra point tied the game at 28-28 with just over seven minutes remaining to play.

Wisconsin intercepted Adler on each of Missouri's next two possessions. The Badgers converted the second of the two turnovers into a 21-yard touchdown run by Marck Harrison with 5:18 left.

Wisconsin led 35-28 when the Tigers' Vernon Boyd scored on a six-yard run with 1:28 left. Missouri went for two points on the conversion, but quarterback Warren Seitz's pass to Shorthose was incomplete.

"This might be better than Bo Derek," Badger coach Dave McClain told the *Wisconsin State Journal* after the game when he was asked to rank the win from one to 10 with the sex symbol/actress being a 10. "Is that possible?"

Johnson shone brightly among several Badger stars that day. He set a school record with three blocks (one extra-point attempt and two punts), intercepted a pass and, of course, returned a blocked punt for a touchdown that started Wisconsin's remarkable fourth-quarter comeback.

Three First-Rounders

Twenty-three Wisconsin players were selected in the first round of the National Football League draft between 1937 and 2005. Only

The great Al Toon was one of three first-round draft choices from Wisconsin in 1985.
Photo courtesy of UW Athletic Communications

once during that 68-year period, however, did three Badgers go in the first round of the same draft.

Head coach Dave McClain's 1984 Badgers put together the school's fourth straight seven-win season and qualified for the Hall of Fame Bowl in Birmingham, Alabama. Three stars from that team heard their names called in the first round on draft day in 1985.

Al Toon, Wisconsin's career leader in receptions and receiving yards until Lee Evans broke both marks in 2003, went to the New York Jets with the 10th pick overall. Cornerback Richard Johnson, who blocked a school-record eight kicks during his career, was chosen by the Houston Oilers with the very next selection. Daryl Sims, who once owned school records for quarterback sack yardage in a season and quarterback sacks in a game, was chosen by the Pittsburgh Steelers with the 20th overall pick.

The Day the Circus Came to Town

In South Bend, Indiana, Notre Dame defensive coordinator Barry Alvarez was celebrating the Fighting Irish's thrilling 31-30 victory over No. 1-ranked Miami. In Los Angeles, Dodgers fans were watching an injured Kirk Gibson hit a dramatic, game-winning home run in the bottom of the ninth inning to give his team a 5-4 victory over Oakland in the first game of the World Series. That same day, October 15, 1988, Camp Randall Stadium played host to "Circus Day."

Head coach Don Morton's Badgers had lost their first five games and were headed toward a 1-10 season. Attendance at Camp Randall Stadium was waning. So, in an effort to liven things up, Mike Leckrone, director of the Wisconsin Band, decided a halftime show based on circus music would be in order.

Clowns, circus wagons and other items were brought in to give the show a circus feel. But Leckrone wanted more. "I had the bright idea that we had to have animals, and I thought it would be the greatest thing in the world to ride an elephant into the stadium," he said. In fact, he got more than he bargained for.

Toward the end of the halftime show, Leckrone got on the elephant and rode down the ramp onto the field and stopped at the 50-yard line. That's when the animal made his mark.

"The elephant stooped down to let me down and then he dropped a pile right on the 50-yard line," Leckrone recalled years later. "I was facing the crowd and I heard a roar. I didn't know what was going on until I looked around and there it was."

The start of the second half was delayed because the UW maintenance staff had to bring a hose out onto the field to clean off the mess.

Incidentally, despite trailing just 7-6 at halftime, the Badgers lost to the Fighting Illini, 34-6.

A Sliver of Light

The three-year (1987-1989) Don Morton coaching era at Wisconsin may have produced just six wins (none of them on the road) in 33 tries, but one of those victories was a big one and continued a trend that started in 1981.

Wisconsin had lost 21 straight games to Ohio State when the two teams faced each other at Camp Randall Stadium in 1981. The Badgers won that game, 24-21, and proceeded to win three of their next five meetings with the Buckeyes. Wisconsin's 1987 team, however, carried a 2-6 overall record and 0-5 Big Ten mark into its November 7 home game with Ohio State, the preseason pick to win the conference title.

But the Badgers got four field goals from Todd Gregoire and were aided by seven Ohio State turnovers in a 26-24 victory. It was Morton's third win at Wisconsin. He would win just three more times in his last two seasons.

"We got some interceptions and some fumbles, and we got Todd Gregoire into a position to help us," Morton said of the win over the Buckeyes. "Then we just held on. Football is a funny game. It's a game of emotion and momentum, and we were able to get something going today."

The Buckeyes, on the other hand, were thoroughly embarrassed and disgusted with their performance.

"We played tough out there, and we moved the ball," said Ohio State coach Earle Bruce, whose team held a 514-233 advantage in total offense. "We just didn't put it away. I'm tremendously upset. I don't even want to think about it. I can't believe it, and I can't explain it."

A True Friend of the Program

In college athletics, the phrase "friend of the program" has sometimes been used as a euphemism for unscrupulous boosters who provide things like money or quasi-employment in violation of NCAA rules. In the case of Father Mike Burke, a longtime friend of the Badger football program, just the opposite is true.

"He was a huge part of my time at Wisconsin," former Badger quarterback Brooks Bollinger said of Burke. "He brings everyone together even though everyone is not Catholic. College athletes go through a lot of tough situations, and he is there to help. He means a lot to so many people. I ended up attending his church on Sundays."

The oldest of eight children born and raised on a dairy farm in Darlington, Wisconsin, Burke was ordained a Catholic priest in 1974 after six years at St. Francis Seminary in Milwaukee. He joined Holy Name Seminary in Middleton, Wisconsin, in 1977.

"My involvement with the football program started at Holy Name [where the Badgers conducted preseason training camp each year] in 1977," Burke said. "The team had a service, and I helped out a few times. It just evolved from there."

Burke spent 18 years at Holy Name before heading to Rome to study for six months. Upon his return he joined the parish at St. Maria Goretti Catholic Church in Madison.

"It has been an interesting and rewarding experience," Burke says of his interaction with the Badger football team. "I've probably done about 75 weddings of football players over the years. It's a different thing than what I do as a priest in the parish."

Burke holds an optional service for the Badgers at home and on the road each morning before their games. "Nobody is required to be there, but it is amazing to see how the teams come together and focus," Burke says.

"He is just someone who helps ground you," head coach Barry Alvarez said of Burke. "He is someone you feel comfortable around, and he is someone over the years that the players have been able to go to with any issues. He's been a friend and a counselor to our players, and he's probably one of my closest friends. He's someone I can always confide in and rely on and bounce things off of and share things with."

CHAPTER NINE

1990-1995

Wisconsin's hiring of head coach Barry Alvarez from Notre Dame in 1990 signaled what would become the greatest and most stable era in the school's football history. Alvarez quickly turned the program around, winning the 1993 Big Ten championship and 1994 Rose Bowl just three seasons after his first team had won just one game. In addition, attendance at Camp Randall Stadium skyrocketed, and it has not dipped since.

Awakening a Sleeping Giant

Most college football programs have, throughout their long histories, experienced up-and-down cycles, periods of success and failure. By the late 1980s, the Badger football program had dipped to one of the true low points in its history.

Following Dave McClain's death after the 1985 season, Wisconsin proceeded to go 9-36 (.200) overall and just 5-27 in Big Ten games during the next four years. The attendance average at Camp Randall Stadium plummeted from 71,613 in 1985 to just 41,734 in 1989. The job as head coach of the Badgers would not have seemed to be an attractive one, but Barry Alvarez thought otherwise.

"I had recruited the Big Ten area," said Alvarez, an assistant coach at Iowa and Notre Dame prior to taking over at Wisconsin in 1990. "I had been in Wisconsin recruiting. I felt I had a good grasp on what needed to be done, and I always felt that a state with one major university had an advantage over schools where there are two major universities (like Iowa and Iowa State or Michigan and Michigan State) competing for the players in that state. I just felt that if it was run right, there was no reason why this shouldn't be a good job. I felt like I had some answers for the job."

Alvarez did, indeed, have some answers for the job. He went on to coach the Badgers to more victories than anyone else in school history and won three Big Ten titles and three Rose Bowls in his first 15 years.

"Get Your Tickets, Now!"

Wisconsin set what was then a home football attendance record in 1984 when an average of 74,681 fans per game watched the Badgers at Camp Randall Stadium. Just five years later, however, that figure had plummeted to 41,734, the school's lowest average since 1945. A cumulative 6-27 record from 1987-1989 had kept the Badger faithful away in droves.

Then, on January 2, 1990, Barry Alvarez was introduced at a press conference as the Badgers' new head coach. The former Iowa and Notre Dame assistant came across as a man with a plan, someone who had been around successful programs and knew how to win. One of his most memorable (and prophetic) comments was directed at Wisconsin football fans.

"But let me say this: they better get season tickets right now, because before long they won't be able to," Alvarez stated that day.

By 1994 the Badgers had sold 58,121 *season tickets*. That figure dipped below 60,000 just twice from 1995-2004, and as of the end of the 2004 season, Camp Randall Stadium had played host to 75 consecutive crowds of 70,000 or more.

Barry Alvarez was the architect of the turnaround in Badger football fortunes during the 1990s. *Photo by David Stluka*

Alvarez's program built such a strong following that Camp Randall Stadium was renovated between 2002-2005, an expansion that included the addition of 72 private suites, 925 club seats, and new permanent south end zone seating, all of which sold out prior to the 2004 season.

Before the Turnaround

Joe Rudolph remembers what it was like. The Belle Vernon, Pennsylvania, native recalls the early days of the Barry Alvarez era at Wisconsin.

"When I first got to Wisconsin [in 1990] nobody would wear their issued gear," Rudolph says. "We were made fun of by everyone, even some of our professors. People would talk about how the games weren't any good, but that at least they could enjoy the band."

Rudolph, a four-year letterwinner as a guard and a team captain in 1994, can also recollect a conversation between his mother and father.

"I can remember my mom telling my dad that someday he wouldn't be able to find a seat at Camp Randall," Rudolph recalled. "Then, years later during the 1993 Ohio State game, my dad stood up to cheer at one point and when he went to sit back down there were so many people in the stands that his seat had disappeared."

Badgers Become Crimefighters

Sophomore fullback Kevin Ellison and sophomore defensive back Dennis Tillman got the 1990 football season off to a good start, in spite of the fact the Badgers lost their opening game, 28-12, to California.

A week before the Barry Alvarez era opened against Cal, Ellison and Tillman were visiting some female friends at one of the women's apartments. The Badger players noticed that the apartment had been ransacked. Drawers were flung open and clothing was strewn about.

Then one of the young women called for help. Tillman and Ellison found a man hiding under the bed and restrained him until the police arrived. The players eventually found out they had apprehended a 28-year-old man wanted in connection with the raping and stabbing of a 12-year-old girl in Florida.

The television show *America's Most Wanted* ended up filming a segment on Ellison and Tillman. "Just seeing yourself on TV and millions of people watching it seems kind of funny," Ellison told the *Milwaukee Sentinel*. "Now my teammates are ragging me about it and calling me 'hero.'"

Shalala Was a Key Figure

One of the key figures in the turnaround of the Badger football program during the early years of the Barry Alvarez era never even worked in the Department of Athletics. Rather, she oversaw it.

Chancellor Donna Shalala, who later became President Bill Clinton's Health and Human Services Secretary, came to Wisconsin in 1988 and found an athletic department in disarray. She endeavored to change that first by hiring Pat Richter as director of athletics. Richter then hired Alvarez, who actually lived in Shalala's home for a short time after his arrival in Madison.

"She was someone who wanted to get things done," Alvarez says of Shalala. "She really had a strong belief that this was a world-class university academically and there was no reason why it couldn't be a world-class university athletically. She really cared about the students and she wanted a good athletic program. She was right in the middle of recruiting with us and we used her help. She wanted us to be successful in athletics, and she did everything she could to help us."

Richter's Magic

The once-downtrodden Wisconsin athletic department got a jolt of life in the late 1980s with the hiring of University Chancellor Donna Shalala. The future U.S. Secretary of Health and Human

Services then hired Badger sports legend Pat Richter as director of athletics. Richter took it from there.

Richter displayed a remarkable ability to hire coaches. Among those he brought to Madison were men's basketball coaches Stu Jackson, Dick Bennett, and Bo Ryan, as well as men's hockey coach Mike Eaves, women's hockey coach Mark Johnson, and volleyball coaches John Cook and Pete Waite. All have been huge successes.

But football coach Barry Alvarez will always be Richter's signature hire. It was Alvarez's success that jump-started not only the football program, but the athletic department in the early 1990s.

"Pat and I had a unique relationship," Alvarez said after he had become Richter's successor as well as the head football coach. "We got along from the very first time we met. We liked each other. He turned the football program over to me and never questioned anything we tried to do. He was an administrator who let his people coach."

Alvarez vs. Wisconsin

Badger head coach Barry Alvarez was a linebacker at Nebraska from 1965-1967 and led the Cornhuskers in tackles his final season.

Alvarez's career included a pair of games against Wisconsin. The No. 2-ranked Cornhuskers blanked the Badgers 37-0 in Lincoln, Nebraska, on October 9, 1965, and then defeated Wisconsin 31-3 at Camp Randall Stadium a year later. Alvarez intercepted a John Ryan pass and returned it 25 yards in that second meeting.

Don Davey

The operative word when describing Wisconsin defensive lineman Don Davey was, simply, "special."

A native of Manitowoc, Wisconsin, Davey joined the Badgers as a freshman in 1986. He played for three different head coaches and endured a low period in the school's football history as

Wisconsin went 10-46 from 1986-1990. But Davey persevered to become one of the most successful student-athletes the football program has ever had.

"Don Davey is a guy I would like to have had on any one of our teams," head coach Barry Alvarez recalled years later. "He would have been a standout on any of our championship teams. I can remember coming in one Sunday and replaying some plays and telling the rest of the guys to watch Don Davey play. He was really special."

A mechanical engineering major, he remains the only four-time, first-team Academic All-American (as selected by the College Sports Information Directors of America) in university division history. He twice was selected by Honda as its scholar-athlete of the year.

Known for his tenacity and relentless effort on the field, Davey started the last 42 games of his career and left Wisconsin as the school record-holder for tackles for loss in a season (24) and career (49). He was a first-team All-Big Ten choice, won Wisconsin's Jimmy Demetral Award (MVP), and was a captain on Alvarez's first team in 1990.

Meeting "Crazylegs"

Jim Hueber has spent 30 years patrolling the sidelines as an assistant football coach. The past 21 years have been in the Big Ten Conference, including the past 13 coaching running backs and offensive linemen at Wisconsin. He has coached in a dozen bowl games and has worked with scores of star players. He would, it might seem, be tough to impress.

But we all have heroes we idolized as kids, and Hueber was no different.

"Growing up as an East Coast kid, I always knew who Elroy Hirsch was, but to go up to him and shake his hand and have a beer with him at Butch's Bologna Bash [an athletic fundraising event at Wisconsin for many years] was a big deal to me," the veteran coach said. "He was a genuine, down-to-Earth guy, and a man of the people of Wisconsin. I had never met him before I worked at Wisconsin. Being able to walk up and shake hands with him, I was like a little kid."

Low Expectations

The level of expectation for the Wisconsin football program, which won six games from 1987-1989, had dipped considerably by the time Barry Alvarez arrived as head coach in 1990. First-year assistant coach John Palermo found out just how low the bar had been set at halftime of the 1991 season-opener.

"We were losing to Western Illinois [a Division I-AA program that had won its season-opener against Washburn the week before] and Barry and I were running off the field at halftime," Palermo recalled. "We're getting beat and the student section is chanting, 'Barry, Barry, Barry.' I looked at Barry and said, 'How about this?' We're losing to Western Illinois, and they're chanting your name!"

Wisconsin went on to defeat the Leathernecks, 31-13.

One Small Step for The Badgers

Wisconsin's third victory of the Barry Alvarez era would not seem, in retrospect, to have had much meaning. After all, Alvarez went on to lead the Badgers to three Big Ten titles on his way to becoming the school's most successful coach. But Wisconsin's 7-6 victory over Iowa State on September 21, 1991, was, indeed, significant.

When Wisconsin took the field that day against the Cyclones, it had been 17 games since the program had defeated an opponent from a league other than the Mid-American Conference. The Badgers had won their 1991 season opener over Division I-AA Western Illinois, but needed to erase a 13-10 halftime deficit to do so. Defeating an opponent from the Big Eight Conference would be a feather in the cap of Alvarez's young program.

The low-scoring game, one that Wisconsin teams were accustomed to finding a way to lose, came down to an Iowa State field goal attempt with 15 seconds left to play. Instead of enduring a 9-7 loss, however, the Badgers blocked the field goal try when linebacker Brendan Lynch pushed an Iowa State player into the kick attempt.

"I can't express how proud I am," Alvarez said after the game. "There was a lot of believing and fighting through adversity out there. I've been in a lot of big wins in my day, but this ranks right up there with any of them."

Vincent's Returns

Victories were hard to come by for head coach Barry Alvarez's first Wisconsin team in 1990, but the Badgers started the 1991 campaign with three straight wins (UW was 3-0 for the first time

All-American Troy Vincent *Photo courtesy of UW Athletic Communications*

since 1985). The first of those triumphs came courtesy of the great Troy Vincent.

The Badgers were facing NCAA Division I-AA opponent Western Illinois in front of just 42,861 fans at Camp Randall Stadium. The Leathernecks had won a 42-3 decision over Washburn the week before. Western Illinois head coach Randy Ball said before the game that he hoped his team could "maintain our composure against a Big Ten team." For a while, they did.

The teams played a scoreless first quarter before the Leathernecks put together a 13-play, 77-yard scoring drive for a 7-0 lead early in the second quarter. They took advantage of a Badger turnover and scored again just over three minutes later to grab a 13-0 advantage.

Wisconsin managed to pull within 13-10 at halftime and took the lead for good on a 13-yard touchdown pass from Tony Lowery to Lee DeRamus early in the third quarter. Western Illinois then punted on its next possession, and Vincent proceeded to bring it back a school-record 90 yards for a touchdown.

"Troy Vincent is one of the best I've ever seen," Ball said. "[His returns] turned the tide of the game."

Vincent returned four punts that day for 146 yards (third most in school history), as well as two kickoffs for 95 yards. The Badgers went on to win 31-13.

Streaks Stop in Minneapolis

Wisconsin's final road game of the 1991 season, at Minnesota, came with extra baggage. The Badgers had followed their 3-0 start with six consecutive defeats. They were riding a 19-game losing streak in conference games and had lost 23 straight contests away from home.

The game started well for the Badgers, who moved out to a 16-0 lead late in the second quarter. But Minnesota chipped away at the Wisconsin lead and tied the game at 16-16 on Mike Chalberg's 32-yard field goal with 11:41 left to play in the game.

Freshman Lee DeRamus's 50-yard kickoff return, however, set the Badgers up at Minnesota's 32-yard line. They ended up with a 42-yard field goal from Rich Thompson and a 19-16 lead.

Minnesota's final possession began at its 18-yard line with 6:32 remaining to play. The Golden Gophers made five first downs as they drove to the Badgers' six-yard line. A five-yard penalty left Minnesota with fourth-and-goal from the Wisconsin 11-yard line with 16 seconds left. That's when Melvin Tucker etched his name into Alvarez era lore.

"They threw a crossing route to their big tight end, and Melvin Tucker just unloaded on him, really a great hit," Alvarez recalled years later of his safety's collision with Patt Evans, Minnesota's intended receiver on the play. "The ball flew the other way, and that iced the ball game."

Moments later the Badgers raced across the Metrodome field to secure the Paul Bunyan Axe, emblematic of the winner of the annual Wisconsin-Minnesota game, for the first time in three years.

The Axe Expert

As Wisconsin's home game with Minnesota approached in mid-November of 1992, head coach Barry Alvarez asked first-year assistant Jim Hueber to address the Badger players.

Hueber had come to Wisconsin after an eight-year stint as an assistant at Minnesota, and Alvarez wanted his players to hear the dual perspective that Hueber could provide about the Badgers-Golden Gophers rivalry and the significance of Paul Bunyan's Axe, which annually goes to the winner of the game between the two schools.

Hueber's annual talk to the Badgers is filled with facts about wins, losses and the personalities that have populated the series between the two schools, which is the most-played in NCAA Division I football (114 meetings through the 2004 season). It is also filled with colorful tales.

"I probably took it a little too far," Hueber said, smiling. "I got into Babe the Blue Ox and Paul Bunyan dragging the axe to start the

The famed Paul Bunyan Axe goes to the winner of the Wisconsin-Minnesota game each year. *Photo by David Stluka*

Mississippi River. But they wanted me to do it again the next year, so I found some other stuff."

Some of that "other stuff" includes the story of Golden Gopher Pug Lund, an All-America running back during the early 1930s. Lund, a native of Rice Lake, Wisconsin, had damaged the little finger on his left hand in Minnesota's 1934 spring game. As the summer wore on, Lund did not feel the finger was getting better so he decided to have it amputated. It healed well enough for Lund to not miss any practice. Hueber's presentation to the Badgers has Lund rationalizing that "it's better to lose a finger than to fumble the ball."

Badgers Clear Another Hurdle

When Wisconsin stepped onto the field at Camp Randall Stadium on October 3, 1992 for its game with 12th-ranked Ohio State, the Badgers did so with the knowledge that their last three wins over nationally ranked opponents had come against the Buckeyes. The most recent of those, however, was in 1985.

The Badgers trailed 10-3 at halftime before taking command in the second half and serving further notice that the program's turnaround under third-year head coach Barry Alvarez was real.

Wisconsin took the second-half kickoff and marched 78 yards in 13 plays as running back Brent Moss scored from five yards out to tie the game at 10-10. Linebacker Gary Casper intercepted a Kirk Herbstreit pass on the next Ohio State possession. This time the Badgers drove 58 yards in 11 plays, with Moss scoring on a three-yard touchdown run. Wisconsin added a 31-yard field goal from Rich Thompson midway through the fourth quarter for a 20-10 lead.

Ohio State scored on its next possession, but failed on a two-point conversion. The Badgers held on for a 20-16 victory.

"It was our first upset, our first big win, and you have to do that to turn a program around," Alvarez said years later about the victory.

Wisconsin's defense limited Ohio State to 45 net yards rushing and 261 yards in total offense. The Badgers also held the ball more than 10 minutes longer than Ohio State.

Payback

When Joe Panos arrived on the Wisconsin campus in 1990, the Badger football program was not held in high regard around the Big Ten. Panos remembers finding that out in the 1991 Ohio State game in Columbus.

"An Ohio State player, Greg Smith, told me during the game, 'You ----, that's why you go to Wisconsin,'" Panos recalled.

The following year, however, when the 12th-ranked Buckeyes came to Camp Randall Stadium, Panos and the Badgers made a statement of their own. "That's one game, I talked way too much," Panos later told *Badger Plus*. "I'm sure he [Smith] didn't remember what he had said. But I yelled at him from play one."

Wisconsin upset Ohio State, 20-16, for the program's first victory over a nationally ranked opponent since 1985.

Why Not Wisconsin?

Every team needs leadership. It needs an individual or a small group that the rest can look up to and follow. The 1993 Badgers were no different, and there was no question as to who the leader of that team was.

"Joe Panos was probably the best leader that I've been around," head coach Barry Alvarez said. "His personality and what he brought to our program had as much to do with us turning it around as anybody. He was tough. We had an incident with a few of our players one summer and he came in and told me he would handle it. If guys were too loud at breakfast, he told them to shut up. He took that leadership role seriously. The players didn't mess with Joe, and they didn't question Joe."

Panos, who is of Greek descent and whose given name is Zois Panagiotopolous, took the hard road to Madison. Virtually unknown to big-time college football recruiters as a senior tight end and defensive lineman at Brookfield (Wisconsin) East High School, Panos contacted the coaching staff at Division III UW-Whitewater and joined the team in 1989.

Panos, however, had bigger dreams. He transferred to UW-Madison, sat out the 1990 campaign (the first of the Alvarez era) and went on to start nine games (five at center and four at right guard) in 1991. The following season he earned second-team All-Big Ten acclaim after starting 11 games at right tackle.

It was during the 1993 season, however, that everything came together for both Panos and the Badgers. "He was a tough guy, who worked hard," said fellow offensive lineman Joe Rudolph. "He was sort of typical of that 1993 team. He had a grab-your-lunch pail-and-hard hat mentality. He was someone you could watch and learn from and emulate."

Joe Panos (58) was a captain and key leader for the Badgers' 1993 Big Ten title team.
Photo courtesy of UW Athletic Communications

Panos started the entire 1993 season (one in which the Badgers finished 10-1-1 and won both the Big Ten and Rose Bowl titles) at right tackle and earned second-team All-America honors. A team cocaptain, he anchored an offensive line that averaged 250.8 yards rushing and 455.2 yards in total offense per game, both tops in the Big Ten.

"Coach Alvarez said I had been voted a captain almost unanimously," Panos recalled. "He wanted me to take care of the team and to take care of things. I hung out with anyone on our team. We were a big family. I wanted my teammates to know that I didn't think I was above anyone else. I would have taken a bullet for those guys."

Following the Badgers' victory in their 1993 Big Ten opener at Indiana, Panos was asked about the possibility of Wisconsin contending for the conference title. He uttered a response now secure in Badger football lore: "Why not Wisconsin?" Later in that unforgettable season, Panos played a big role in saving the lives of several UW students who were injured during the infamous postgame "crush" after the victory over Michigan at Camp Randall Stadium.

He went on to a seven-year career in the National Football League with Philadelphia and Buffalo.

"I think he changed everything about the team when he came here," longtime Badger assistant coach Jim Hueber said. "He was a walk-on who came from nothing. I remember his toughness and the way he did things. He enjoyed success, but he came from nothing."

Badgers Bite Back

In a championship season filled with memorable games and moments, Wisconsin's 24-16 victory at SMU on September 11, 1993, would not seem on the surface to have mattered much at all. In reality, however, it could be argued that the win over the Mustangs was the final rung on the Badgers climb back to respectability.

Wisconsin had begun the fourth season of the Barry Alvarez era by knocking off Nevada, 35-17, in the season-opener at Camp Randall Stadium. However, all but one of Alvarez's nine wins as the Badgers' head coach up to that point had occurred at home. In fact, Wisconsin had just one road win to its credit in the past seven seasons. Each game outside of Madison was a challenge.

The Badgers traveled to Dallas where the gametime temperature was 94 degrees. "We have since figured out a schedule for night games," Alvarez recalled years later. "But we got there and it was really hot, and we lay around in the hotel all day. Then we got to the stadium and it was basically a high school locker room. We walked across a parking lot and a street [to get to the field]!"

Despite playing the Mustangs to something of a statistical draw, Wisconsin fell behind 13-0 at the half, conjuring up images of numerous past failures on the road.

To add injury to insult, SMU's mascot decided to use the fingers of a Badger volunteer staffer for a halftime snack. Pat O'Connor had gone over to the pony's handler and asked to pet the animal. The horse turned and chomped on O'Connor's hand, drawing blood. O'Connor, however, was not hurt seriously and he, like the Badgers, bounced back for the second half.

Wisconsin took the second-half kickoff, drove to SMU's 26-yard line, and came away with a 44-yard field goal from John Hall. The Mustangs responded with a field goal of their own before the Badgers pulled within 16-10 after an 80-yard scoring drive ended with a one-yard touchdown run by Brent Moss at the end of the third quarter.

Moss spearheaded the Badgers' attack in the second half, gaining 107 of his 181 rushing yards after halftime. Quarterback Darrell Bevell hit J.C. Dawkins with a 25-yard scoring strike with 6:28 remaining in the fourth quarter, giving Wisconsin the lead for good.

"I'm very proud of this team," Alvarez said afterward. "They looked adversity in the eye and handled it."

The Associated Press poll the following week showed the Badgers at No. 24, the school's first national ranking since October of 1981. Wisconsin went on to a 10-1-1 record, the school's first Big Ten title in 30 years and the UW's first Rose Bowl victory. The breakthrough campaign featured six wins away from Camp Randall Stadium, a sure sign the program was on its way.

Wanted: One Yard

A strong argument could be made that running back was the signature offensive position at Wisconsin during the Alvarez era. Four of the school's top five career rushing leaders played for Alvarez, including Ron Dayne, the 1999 Heisman Trophy winner and college football's all-time leading ground-gainer, Anthony Davis, Brent Moss, and Terrell Fletcher.

Badger fans would probably be curious to know which of those illustrious backs would get the ball if Alvarez and his staff were told they needed just one yard.

"Barry and I have been asked that question and we both have the same answer: Brent Moss," said Jim Hueber, who coached the running backs (including Moss and Fletcher) and later the offensive line under Alvarez. "We called him the 'Alley Cat.' For one yard, there was nobody that was going to get him down. He would fight, scratch, find a way. For one yard, he was the guy you wanted with the ball."

Alvarez, who confirmed Hueber's sentiment by calling Moss "the best finisher we've had," also remembers Moss's toughness.

"I remember we were playing Purdue when Brent and 'Fletch' [running back Terrell Fletcher] were alternating playing time," Alvarez recounted. "Brent knew that if Fletch got too much playing time, he might take his job. Moss got hit and knocked out on a play right in front of us. Fletch went in and finished the series, but the next series Moss was pulling on my arm to go back in. He had been knocked out, but he just flat told the doctors he was going back in. He didn't want to lose his spot."

Moss was named the Big Ten MVP in 1993 and earned the same honor at the 1994 Rose Bowl. His 312 carries and 1,637 rushing yards in 1993 were both single-season school records that

Brent Moss (33) was the 1993 Big Ten MVP. *Photo courtesy of UW Athletic Communications*

have since been eclipsed. He is the school's fourth-leading rusher with 3,428 yards.

"He ran harder than anyone I ever played with, including my years in the NFL," former Badger offensive tackle Joe Panos said. "It made us want to hold our blocks that much longer."

Wrong Number

Wisconsin's 4-0 start and the excitement it generated early in the 1993 season had an unintended effect on a company some 3,000 miles away.

Badger fans, enthused about the program's success and anxious to purchase tickets to Wisconsin home games, did what anyone would do. They called the UW Athletic Ticket Office at (800) GO BADGERS. Well, most of them did.

It seems The Badge Company of Huntington Beach, Calfornia, which sold identification badges and plaques, had a toll-free phone line for its customers. That number was (800) BADGES 7.

Kristen Blankinship, the company's production manager, said her firm was being inundated with phone calls from Wisconsin football fans looking for tickets. "Our customers couldn't get through to us," Blankinship told *The Milwaukee Journal*. "We had calls the last three seasons, but nothing like this."

A Chance to Say 'Thanks'

Two days after 76 people had been injured during the infamous "crowd surge" following the Badgers' 13-10 victory over Michigan at Camp Randall Stadium on October 30, 1993, Steve Malchow, then Wisconsin's men's sports information director, was visiting with reporters from three national newspapers when the phone in his office rang.

"There was a young lady on the other end of the line who said she was a student at the Michigan game," Malchow recalled. "She said she had been getting crushed in the stampede and that 'number three' had saved her life."

The stampede to which Aimee Jansen was referring had occurred when thousands of students surged forward in an effort to come out of the stands and onto the field to celebrate the win over the Wolverines. What happened instead was students were hemmed in against railings and fences that eventually gave way. Bodies stacked upon each other as many students struggled to breathe.

After visiting some more with Jansen, Malchow concluded that "number three" was Michael Brin, a walk-on sophomore receiver. Jansen asked Malchow if he could help her contact Brin to thank him. Ed Sherman of the *Chicago Tribune*, Malcolm Moran of *The New York Times* and Gene Wojciechowski of the *Los Angeles Times* sat in Malchow's office listening to the conversation.

"I told [Jansen] that I had reporters from three of the biggest newspapers in the United States in my office at that moment, and I asked her if she would visit with them over the speakerphone," Malchow said. "She agreed. A terrible situation wound up creating some incredible stories."

Jansen proceeded to tell the reporters the story of how she had been crushed in the sea of bodies and how Brin had helped her out of the crowd. She told them Brin had saved her life.

Fortunately for Jansen, Brin had by chance remained on the field to look for friends in the stands. That's when he spotted her and others in distress. Brin and teammates Joe Panos, Tyler Adam, John Hall, and Brent Moss, among others, helped save several students that day. Brin, who was named ABC's Newsmaker of the Week, finally met Jansen a few days later.

"They Never Had a Chance"

It was on the bus ride from the team hotel to Illinois's Memorial Stadium that Joe Panos knew.

Head coach Barry Alvarez had just informed the Badgers that Michigan had defeated Ohio State, 28-0. "Coach Alvarez told us that Michigan had just beaten Ohio State, and that if we beat Illinois we controlled our own destiny. They never had a chance."

Panos was right. The Badgers steamrolled the Fighting Illini, 35-10, and outgained their hosts by a 523-227 margin in total offense. The victory put the Big Ten title in Wisconsin's hands, and they did not let it slip away. Two weeks later the Badgers defeated Michigan State, 41-20, in Tokyo, to lock up their first Rose Bowl bid in 31 years.

Tokyo

If you had asked Barry Alvarez where he thought he might win his first Big Ten championship as coach of the Badgers, chances are pretty good Tokyo would not have been his answer.

The Tokyo Dome, known as the "Big Egg," however, is exactly where it took place.

"When we first set it up a year in advance, a lot of people figured it would more or less be our bowl trip," then director of athletics Pat Richter recalled. "Then to have the game go like it did, to win it, to have the Rose Bowl people there to present the roses, then it all started to sink in."

Alvarez left nothing to chance as he tried to prepare his team to face Michigan State halfway around the world. He had the Badger players managing their body clocks, wearing sunglasses during the day and staying up later at night.

"The day before we left, we practiced from 9-11 p.m.," Alvarez said. "We went to a midnight movie, got on a bus and drove to Chicago. I told the guys they couldn't sleep until they got to the hotel. They slept until noon, went to the airport and I told them they could not sleep on the flight to Tokyo. We were on the same flight with Michigan State and our guys felt like they had an edge because they saw Michigan State's players, who had just played the day before, falling asleep as the plane took off."

One of the best experiences the team had in Tokyo was the time they spent with Wisconsin alumni.

"We had contacted our alumni, some were Japanese, some were Americans working over there," Alvarez remembered. "They each were responsible for a few of our players for one night. Some took them to their homes to eat, some to restaurants, some showed them around the city. Our players enjoyed it."

Wisconsin fell behind 7-3 after the first quarter, but bounced back to take a 24-7 lead at halftime thanks to two second-quarter touchdown runs by Terrell Fletcher and another from Brent Moss. The Badgers went on to win, 41-20, rolling up 521 yards in total offense. Moss (147) and Fletcher (112) each gained more than 100 yards.

"I was numb afterward, just floating," Alvarez recalled. "Pat [Richter] and I [and a group of close friends] ended up eating at a Tony Roma's. We ran into several Michigan State players who congratulated us on the game."

Richter remembered the feeling of dreamlike disbelief. "It was surreal," he said. "Leaving Japan, the long flight, the people recognizing what happened on the bus ride home. You had to kind of pinch yourself. We didn't know what it would be like, but it sure felt good."

The Bus Ride Back

The Badgers' bus ride from Chicago's O'Hare Airport back to Madison was the final leg of their return trip from Tokyo after their Rose Bowl-clinching, 41-20 victory over Michigan State in December of 1993. It was one of the most memorable parts of the entire Tokyo experience.

Particularly once the team's buses crossed the state line from Illinois into Wisconsin, fans started to realize that the Badgers were on those buses.

"We landed at O'Hare Airport, drove up I-90, and when we got to the first Wisconsin exit there was a man and his son sitting in the back of a pickup truck with a sign that said 'Welcome Home to Our Heroes,'" recalled John Chadima, the program's administrative assistant at the time. "Everybody was dumbfounded. It was incredibly emotional."

Assistant coach Jim Hueber has similar memories.

"People were pulling their cars over on overpasses and waving and honking their horns and trying to ride beside us," recalled Hueber.

Chadima had called ahead to make sure a welcome home celebration had been planned for the Badgers' arrival back at Camp Randall Stadium. Streets were blocked off and there was a police escort from the time the Badgers exited I-90 until they reached the stadium.

"We drove the buses into the stadium, and there were about 40,000 people there, even though it was early December and it was cold outside," Chadima remembered. "'We Are the Champions' was playing. It was an incredible day."

Two Celebrations in Pasadena

For decades the ultimate goal for a Big Ten football player has been to win the conference title and make the trip west to Pasadena, California, to play in the Rose Bowl. By 1993 it had been a dream deferred year after year for the University of Wisconsin's players since the Badgers had last appeared in the game on New Year's Day in 1963.

The 1993 season, however, was different than the previous 30 years in Madison, and as the campaign rolled along, the Badgers played their way into contention for the Big Ten championship.

Scott Nelson, Wisconsin's senior starter at free safety, had been with the program since 1989, the final year of head coach Don Morton's three-year tenure. Nelson had witnessed the transformation of Badger football under Morton's successor, Barry Alvarez, and could appreciate as well as anyone how special the 1993 season was becoming. During that time, however, something else was happening: Nelson's relationship with his girlfriend, Becky Kliefoth, an athletic trainer at Wisconsin, had become increasingly serious.

"The summer before my senior year, I started to feel like this was right," Nelson said of his relationship with Kliefoth, whom he had known since they attended Sun Prairie High School together. "But I had only told my dad what I was thinking about, not my brothers or my mom."

Wisconsin kept winning football games, and Nelson decided he would propose to Kliefoth at whichever bowl game the Badgers played in. He had not imagined it would be the Rose Bowl, but that is precisely what happened after Wisconsin defeated Michigan State in Tokyo to clinch a share of the league crown and berth in Pasadena.

"John Chadima [then Wisconsin's football administrative assistant] and I had worked on figuring out where Becky would be sitting and how we would get her down onto the field, and only if we won," Nelson said.

The Badgers, of course, did win, 21-16, over UCLA. On the field after the game, Nelson was being interviewed by media when he turned around to see Becky standing there near him.

"I go from the emotional high of the victory to enjoying the moment to sort of a complete lack of composure," Nelson said. "I felt the nervousness you feel before a game."

Nelson had given the engagement ring to Father Mike Burke, a Catholic priest from Madison, who had been a friend to the Badger football program and was on the sideline during the game. Burke walked by Nelson and slipped the ring into his hand. The diamond on the ring was a diamond from Nelson's paternal grandmother's ring, a gift from Scott's father.

"I knew I was going to ask her to marry me, but it hadn't really sunk in until Father Mike handed me the ring," Nelson said. "At that point it was like, 'OK, here we go.' I got down on my knee, popped open the box and asked her to marry me. We have a perfect picture of her jaw dropping to the ground. It took her a little while to figure out what was happening, too, but she said yes. It was a night where we celebrated our win and our engagement."

Ashes in the Rose Bowl

Wisconsin's appearance in the 1994 Rose Bowl game was a dream come true for an entire generation of Badger fans who thought they would never see the day the Cardinal and White would return to Pasadena. Mike Leckrone, director of the UW Band since 1969, certainly wondered if he would ever see it.

Thrilled though he was to have been there, however, one of Leckrone's most vivid memories of the experience involved neither the game nor the band's actual musical performance.

It seems the friend of a Wisconsin Band alumnus approached Jim Tanner, one of Leckrone's assistants, as the band was entering the stadium that New Year's Day. He went on to tell Tanner that his father had died, been cremated and wished to have his ashes scattered in the Rose Bowl if the Badgers ever got there. He then handed Tanner a bag containing his father's ashes and asked: "Do you think it could be done?"

Tanner, a minister, put the bag in his pocket, but more or less forgot about it until the Fifth Quarter (the band's well-known, on-the-field postgame show). Tanner felt something in his pocket and remembered that it was the ashes. So, with the band and the Badger fans celebrating the school's 21-16 victory over UCLA, Tanner went to the Wisconsin end zone, spread the ashes around and said a little prayer.

Berry Alvarez

You know you've arrived when you've got an ice cream flavor named after you in a state known as "America's Dairyland."

In 1994, after the Badgers had won their first Rose Bowl, the UW-Madison dairy store at Babcock Hall created a new ice cream flavor, Berry Alvarez, in honor of the coach responsible for the remarkable turnaround of Wisconsin football. Berry Alvarez is a mixture of raspberry, strawberry and blueberry.

DeRamus Arrives

One of the great offensive talents of head coach Barry Alvarez's early years at Wisconsin was wide receiver Lee DeRamus.

DeRamus, who like Ron Dayne after him was from New Jersey and was recruited by Badger assistant coach Bernie Wyatt, set the Wisconsin record for receiving yards in a season with 920 in 1993. Wyatt remembers the day DeRamus showed up on campus.

"Lee came here early, in June," Wyatt recalled. "We were in the old offices at the stadium and we heard the horn of a car beeping outside. I went over to the window, looked out, and there was Lee, with his whole family, in a limousine. They had the top open and I saw Lee with his body halfway out. He looked up at me and yelled, 'I'm here, Coach!'"

DeRamus's career at Wisconsin was cut short when he broke his leg in practice two days before the 1994 season opener against Eastern Michigan. He never played for the Badgers again, instead making himself available for the National Football League draft in the spring of 1995. He was a sixth-round selection of the New Orleans Saints.

Nick Rafko

When coaches, players, and support staff from the early years of the Barry Alvarez era at Wisconsin are asked to recall funny stories or people, they respond with one name: Nick Rafko.

Known for his sense of humor and personality, Rafko was a four-year letterwinner (1990-1993) as a reserve linebacker. He enjoyed his best season, statistically, when he made 25 tackles in 1992, but it was his influence on the program off the field that lives on.

"He was such a good person," remembered teammate Joe Rudolph. "He was always smiling and joking. He was so much a part of the program, and he always had a pulse on what the team needed." Rafko, in fact, was actually one of the acts (along with

Chris Farley and Bob Hope) at the Big Ten Dinner of Champions at the Rose Bowl. He did a Kermit the Frog imitation.

Upon completion of his career, Rafko, whose sister was 1987 Miss America Kaye Lani Rae Rafko, returned home to the Detroit area where he had just started a new job. One day in late June of 1994, Nick dropped his fiancée off at her house after a wedding the pair had attended. A short time later he was killed when the vehicle he was driving collided with a pickup truck at an intersection.

Word of the tragedy made its way back to Madison. A busload of Rafko's former teammates traveled to Michigan for the funeral services. Strength and conditioning coach John Dettmann rode the bus, too.

"When we got on the bus, it was like a normal bunch of guys on a bus, everybody kind of light-hearted, playing games, doing what you'd normally do," Dettmann recalled. "I remember pulling over to a roadside station to change clothes as we got closer to the funeral site. We got back on the bus and you could feel the whole bus was cold. It was intense. You could have cut the air with a knife. It's something I'll never forget."

The bus carrying the Badgers was one of the vehicles in the funeral procession. That fall Rafko's family returned to Madison for a pregame ceremony at which Alvarez and the team captains participated on the field at Camp Randall Stadium.

Good Ones to Learn From

It never hurts to have good teachers. Wisconsin head coach Barry Alvarez is living proof of that fact.

Alvarez played and/or coached for three of college football's legendary head coaches. The first was Nebraska's Bob Devaney, for whom Alvarez played linebacker from 1965-1967. Alvarez was, in fact, the Cornhuskers' leading tackler in 1967, a year in which they led the nation in total defense and created a school-record 40 turnovers.

"Bob was really ahead of his time," Alvarez said. "I really admired how he communicated with people. He was comfortable around all sorts of people, whether it was a mill worker or the governor, and they all seemed to like him. He handled his players well, and the way he went about his business and prepared his team was way ahead of his time."

Alvarez was an assistant to Iowa's Hayden Fry from 1979-1986. The former Hawkeye head coach is fifth on the Big Ten's all-time win list.

"More than anything else, I think everyone who coached at Iowa learned organization from Hayden," Alvarez said. "How to set up a program, run a program, manage a program. Everyone knew what their roles were. He really ran a good program."

Alvarez's last stop before taking over at Wisconsin was a three-year stint as an assistant coach at Notre Dame with head coach Lou Holtz. The Fighting Irish went 32-5 during Alvarez's years there, including winning the 1988 national championship.

"What I took from Lou were probably my football beliefs, some of the fundamentals I believe in and a plan to win a game. I've seen other people try to emulate Lou, but I learned you can't be him; you've got to be yourself. I stole a little bit from each one of those guys."

A Reward for Their Effort

Barry Alvarez took the head coaching position at Wisconsin in 1990 armed with the knowledge that he had his work cut out for him. The program was a combined 9-36 the previous four seasons.

Nonetheless, Alvarez's attempt to turn the program around had to start somewhere, and years later he retained affection for the players who battled through his first season with him.

"We weren't very good," Alvarez recalled of the 1990 season in which the Badgers were 1-10. "We had a lot of guys leave the program, but I was very appreciative of the ones who stayed around. I'll never forget our last game. We were 1-9 and we were playing Michigan State, which was a bowl team, and we had a chance to win. I told them afterward that I appreciated their effort. They battled and they never quit."

Alvarez also delivered on a promise he made to many in that first group of seniors when he presented them each with a Rose Bowl watch after the Badgers' New Year's Day victory over UCLA in 1994.

Bringing Home The Bacon

Will Roleson was a first-year intern in the UW Men's Sports Information Office when he stumbled upon a piece of college football history while cleaning out a storage room in Camp Randall Stadium during the summer of 1994.

"We were cleaning out a storage closet in the stadium, and it was filled with old yearbooks, press releases, and other types of publications," Roleson said. "This leather briefcase caught my eye, because it was so different from everything else in there. I opened up the case and there was the Slab of Bacon. No one really seemed to know what it was."

A creation of R.B. Fouch of Minneapolis, the Slab of Bacon went to the winner of the Wisconsin-Minnesota football game each year from 1930 through some point during the 1940s. The "trophy" is a black walnut slab with the word "BACON" carved at both ends. On one side is a football with an "M" or "W" (depending on how it is displayed) inscribed on it. There is a leather strap at each end.

Peg Watrous, a Wisconsin student during the 1940s, recounted that she and a student from Minnesota were to have exchanged the slab following a game. The Golden Gophers won and, with fans running all over the field, Watrous lost track not only of her counterpart but, eventually, the bacon, too. The unexplained disappearance of the slab resulted in the creation of Paul Bunyan's Axe, the famed trophy for which both schools have competed since 1948.

Despite the fact the slab had been out of the picture since at least the late 1940s, it had the scores of every Badger-Golden Gopher game from 1930-1970 painted on it when Roleson made his discovery. The trophy is now on display in the Wisconsin football offices at Camp Randall Stadium.

"We took home the bacon," Badger coach Barry Alvarez said in 1992, "and kept it."

Not Exactly Sweating It Out

The weekend of the annual National Football League Draft is, of course, normally a time when many players nervously await word on their football futures. Former Badger center Cory Raymer was not one of those players.

Raymer, following the 1994 season during which he became Wisconsin's first consensus All-American in 13 years, was selected by the Washington Redskins in the second round of the 1995 NFL Draft.

Each spring, when the draft rolls around, the University of Wisconsin athletic communications office (formerly sports information) makes recently drafted Badger football players available to the local media either in person or via phone. So sports information director Steve Malchow gathered reporters in his office and called Raymer's home in Fond du Lac, Wisconsin. Raymer's mother answered and called her son to the phone.

"I put Cory on the speakerphone in my office and asked him to tell everyone how he had spent the day while he was waiting to be drafted," Malchow recalled. "Cory says, 'Oh, nothing much, I've just been out back in a creek catching fish barehanded.'"

That's Experience

By the time a college athlete becomes a fifth-year senior, it can seem as if that athlete has been around forever. Former Badger quarterback Darrell Bevell, however, took it to a whole new level.

There was a reason head coach Barry Alvarez joked in August of 1995 that Bevell would be "back for his ninth season at quarterback."

Bevell left Northern Arizona University after redshirting as a freshman in 1989 so that he could spend the next two years in

Darrell Bevell quarterbacked the Badgers to the 1994 Rose Bowl championship.
Photo courtesy of UW Athletic Communications

Cleveland on a Mormon mission. Brad Childress, Northern Arizona's offensive coordinator, eventually took over the same position with the Badgers. Bevell transferred to Wisconsin and became the starter as a 22-year-old freshman in 1992.

Bevell went on to earn first-team All-Big Ten honors during a sophomore year in which he set a school record for pass efficiency (155.2) and helped lead the Badgers to the 1993 Big Ten title and Rose Bowl victory. He finished his career as a 25-year-old senior in 1995.

Stopping the Streak

It would be an understatement to say the 1995 Badgers had drawn a tough assignment when they had to travel to Penn State's Beaver Stadium on September 30 to face the sixth-ranked Nittany Lions under the lights in front of 96,540 fans and millions more watching on ESPN.

Penn State, owner of a nation-leading 20-game winning streak, had not lost a home game since October 16, 1993, and was, of course, under the direction of college football coaching icon Joe Paterno.

Badger head coach Barry Alvarez, however, had told his team earlier in the week that there is nothing like doing something no one thinks you can do. The Badgers took their coach's statement to heart and responded with one of the very best performances of the Alvarez era on their way to a stunning 17-9 victory.

"This was pretty big," Alvarez said afterward. "It was a huge football game. I'm real proud of my kids, the coaching staff for preparing to come into a tough environment against a great football team, playing against a legend. I really liked the way the kids responded. They came in here and just played their hearts out."

Alvarez may have set the tone after the Badgers won the coin toss. He opted to take the ball, and it proved to be a good choice as the Badgers drove 72 yards and took a 3-0 lead on a 26-yard field goal from John Hall.

While the Badgers were getting a remarkably efficient performance from quarterback Darrell Bevell (18-of-22 passing for 192 yards, two touchdowns and no interceptions), the Wisconsin defense was putting the clamps on a potent offense that was averaging 50 points and 531 yards per game and included standout receivers Bobby Engram and Freddie Scott.

Penn State quarterback Wally Richardson set a school record with 33 pass completions (on 48 attempts) but managed to guide his club into the Badger endzone just once on a five-yard pass to Scott with 4:10 remaining to play in the game. Wisconsin had already become the first team to shut out the Nittany Lions in the first half since Miami in 1992.

Among the game's memorable plays was Badger defensive tackle Jason Maniecki's sack of Richardson on the last Penn State drive. Maniecki brought down Richardson and guard Marco Rivera together on the play.

"You've got to give them credit," Paterno said of the Badgers after the game. "I don't know whether they had a penalty (UW actually had two penalties for 10 yards). They made all the third-down plays (the Badgers were 11 of 17 on third down). They just played one heckuva football game."

Don't Mess with The Bull

Defensive tackle Jason Maniecki made 80 tackles in 1995, but his final season as a Badger could be defined by just two of those stops.

Wisconsin's season had begun erratically, with the Badgers taking a 1-1-1 record into their Big Ten opener at sixth-ranked Penn State. The Nittany Lions were riding the nation's longest winning streak at 20 games and would be playing at night in front of 96,540 of their closest friends at legendary Beaver Stadium, as well as a national television audience.

The Badgers, however, played a near-perfect game that ended in a 17-9 upset victory. Quarterback Darrell Bevell completed 18-of-22 passes for 192 yards and two touchdowns to key the offensive effort. Maniecki, who had nine tackles in the win, capped the defensive performance on Penn State's final drive when his "bull rush" resulted in an eight-yard sack of quarterback Wally Richardson (and guard Marco Rivera) on second-and-five at the Badger 35-yard line.

Later in the season the Badgers were battling for their third straight bowl berth when they traveled to Minnesota sporting a 3-4-1 overall mark. Wisconsin led 34-27 when the Golden Gophers took over at their own 45-yard line with 4:15 remaining to play. Quarterback Cory Sauter guided Minnesota to the Wisconsin 20-yard line and a fourth-and-four situation when history repeated itself.

Conjuring up images of his memorable sack at Penn State, Maniecki bulldozed two Golden Gopher linemen into Sauter, toppling the quarterback for a nine-yard loss and effectively ending Minnesota's comeback bid.

Badger linebacker Eric Unverzagt compared Maniecki's two sacks after the game. "This game he only tackled three guys," he told the *Milwaukee Journal Sentinel*. "At Penn State it was more like six. He's a monster, definitely."

Mr. October?

Throughout his tenure at Wisconsin, head coach Barry Alvarez has continually taken advantage of any opportunity he has had to have his teams meet or hear from famous people.

Actors Chris Farley and Henry Winkler, baseball manager Tommy Lasorda, golfer Jerry Kelly, former Notre Dame football player Rudy Reuttiger, sportscaster Bob Costas, and the Reverend Jesse Jackson are just some of the celebrities who have addressed the Badgers since 1990.

Jackson's visit was one of the most memorable. The former presidential candidate was making an appearance in Madison, and Alvarez arranged to have him talk to the Badgers in their locker room in the McClain Center.

Jackson completed his talk and, when he had finished, welcomed the players to ask any questions they might have. The story goes that one of the Badgers signaled that he had a question, and Jackson acknowledged the player.

"How did it feel to hit those three home runs in the World Series and who named you Mr. October?" came the question. The room, of course, erupted in laughter as one of the players had mistaken the Reverend's identity with that of baseball legend Reggie Jackson.

The Wrong Time to Watch

Defensive end Tarek Saleh left Wisconsin with all of the school's records for tackles for loss and quarterback sacks. *The Football News* named him a first-team All-American in 1996, and he was a two-time consensus first-team All-Big Ten selection. But even Saleh had to learn what it took to be successful at Wisconsin.

"Once when he [Saleh] was a freshman, we were out at practice and the offense ran a toss sweep away," recalled defensive line coach John Palermo. "Tarek just kind of stood there and watched the ballcarrier run down the sideline." Those familiar with Palermo's fiery coaching style can imagine what came next.

"Out of the corner of his eye Tarek saw me running out after him, so he took off after the ballcarrier," Palermo said. "I chased him all the way down the field, chewing him out as I went. I said, 'You're not in high school any more; you need to get to the ball!'"

The Imposter

Badger head coach Barry Alvarez has arranged for a number of famous people to talk to his football team over the years, but lining up "President Bill Clinton" to visit practice at Camp Randall Stadium ranks as one of his better efforts.

John Chadima, then the Badger football team's administrative assistant, had driven Alvarez to a meeting on campus over the noon hour, and the two were returning to Camp Randall when Alvarez said to Chadima, "Oh, I forgot to tell you the president is coming to practice today. Make sure security is all set around the stadium and that everything is in place."

Chadima was stunned, but figured that Alvarez must have set it up through former UW Chancellor Donna Shalala, who at the time worked in the Clinton Administration as the U.S. Secretary of Health and Human Services. So Chadima did what he was asked to do. He called various units around the campus and stadium, alerting them to the president's impending visit.

Alvarez, who had told the Badgers they would have a special guest at practice that afternoon, huddled the team in the north end of the field as a limousine pulled into the stadium from the southwest corner.

"I believed it right up until about five minutes before 'Clinton' got there when someone commented to me about what a good one Barry was pulling on the team," Chadima recalled later.

The presidential impersonator spoke to the team for a few minutes before being whisked away by "Secret Service agents."

Special Teams Save the Day

Neither Wisconsin nor Minnesota was having a particularly good season by the time they met in Minneapolis in November of 1995. In fact, each team needed to win to keep its bowl hopes alive. And, of course, the Paul Bunyan Axe was at stake. The Badgers were 3-4-1 overall and 2-3 in Big Ten play. Minnesota was 3-5 overall and 1-4 in league action.

The Badgers won what turned out to be a typically entertaining game between the two rivals, 34-27. What made the victory special for the Badgers, however, was the fact that it included two of the longest plays in school history.

The game was tied 10-10 when Wisconsin's John Hall lined up to attempt a 60-yard field goal with just two seconds left to play in the first half. Hall's kick was good, giving the Badgers a 13-10 lead at the break. The kick broke the Wisconsin school record (54 yards) previously held by Todd Gregoire and was the fourth-longest in modern-era Big Ten history.

The other play took place after Minnesota went ahead 17-13 early in the third quarter. Mike Chalberg kicked off to Wisconsin's Aaron Stecker, who had twice fumbled on returns in a 35-0 loss to Northwestern a few weeks earlier. Stecker caught the ball and raced 100 yards for a touchdown. It was the Badgers' first kickoff return for a touchdown since 1989 and tied the school record held jointly by Ira Matthews and Michael Jones.

Wisconsin lost the next week at home to Iowa and tied Illinois, 3-3, in the season finale. The Badgers did not play in a bowl game that season, but they did have a couple of electrifying special teams plays they could look back on.

CHAPTER TEN

1996-1999

The Ron Dayne Era at Wisconsin was one that fans of the program will remember forever. Wisconsin put together a 37-13 record (including 20-4 at home) and won back-to-back Big Ten and Rose Bowl titles in Dayne's last two seasons. Dayne's final game at Camp Randall Stadium was extraordinarily memorable as he set the Division I career rushing record on a day the Badgers clinched the league title. Head coach Barry Alvarez cemented his spot as the most successful coach in school history, passing Phil King on the all-time Wisconsin wins list after a victory over Michigan State in 1999.

Early Impressions

Credit head coach Barry Alvarez and his staff for seeing something in Ron Dayne that other schools did not see: a tailback.

"I watched high school film of him, and he was lined up at fullback," Alvarez said of the player who would become college football's career rushing leader. "But every once in a while they lined him up at tailback and they'd give him the ball and you could see a burst and you'd see him come out the back end and then you'd see him outrun the secondary. I really thought he could be a good tailback, and we were the only team that recruited him as a tailback."

Dayne, of course, set the NCAA Division I career rushing record in the Badgers' final regular-season game of 1999 (at home against Iowa). A few weeks later he won the Heisman Trophy. Dayne carried 1,220 times for 7,125 yards and 71 touchdowns during his four-year Wisconsin career.

Record Night in Hawaii

Wisconsin's regular-season finale at Hawaii in 1996 was not televised, so only the 26,819 fans in Aloha Stadium saw what happened. It's probably safe to say they will remember it for a long time.

What those fans witnessed was the continuing development of a player who three years later would become college football's career rushing leader. Ron Dayne set the single-game Wisconsin rushing record that night in Honolulu, capping a remarkable rookie season and setting the stage for an amazing career.

"It was like trying to stop a Mack truck with a pea shooter," Hawaii defensive coordinator Don Lindsey told the *Wisconsin State Journal.* "It was no contest. No mas."

The game began in bizarre fashion. The Rainbow Warriors kicked off and were whistled for a personal foul (late hit). The Badgers were then called for four consecutive penalties, including illegal motion on their first play, a 67-yard run by Dayne that was called back. Once the officials put away their whistles, however, Dayne took over.

Dayne rushed for 71 yards on the first play after the stretch of penalties. Two plays later he was in the end zone from four yards out. He carried 36 times for 339 yards and four touchdowns against the Rainbow Warriors that evening and broke Herschel Walker's NCAA record for rushing yards in a season by a freshman.

Dayne went on to add to his total with a 246-yard performance against Utah in the 1996 Copper Bowl. He finished the season with a school-record 2,109 yards.

Rooonnnn Daaayynne!

Mike Mahnke was understandably nervous as he prepared for his first game as public address announcer at Camp Randall Stadium on September 2, 1995. It was to be just the second night game in stadium history, and the 21st-ranked Badgers were hosting No. 13 Colorado in front of a national television audience. In addition, Mahnke's wife, Tonia, was due to deliver the couple's first child that day.

Mahnke could never have imagined that five years later he would become something of a cult figure, linked by Badger fans with 1999 Heisman Trophy winner Ron Dayne.

A native of Racine, Wisconsin, Mahnke is a 1984 graduate of Wisconsin and the vice-president/creative director at Roundhouse Marketing and Promotions in Madison. He started serving as P.A. announcer at Badger women's basketball games in the early 1990s and began doing football and men's basketball after longtime P.A. man Jack Rane died in 1994.

Dayne arrived at Wisconsin in 1996, and by the end of his rookie season it was clear the Badgers had someone special running the ball for them. Mahnke was, of course, there for every carry in Camp Randall, calling out Dayne's name after each one. Mahnke says it was sometime during the 1998 season that a unique sound started coming out of Camp Randall Stadium. Following each carry, the student section in the northeast corner of the stadium would in unison echo Mahnke's musical pronouncement of "Roooonnnn Daaayynne!" By Dayne's final game as a Badger, most of the stadium had joined in the fun.

"It caught me by surprise," Mahnke says. "The P.A. guy is usually a nameless, faceless persona. One of my secrets was that I wouldn't do the full "Ron Dayne thing" unless he gained seven yards or more, or scored a touchdown. It was kind of cool when that took off [with the fans] and I started having some fun with it late in the 1999 season."

Mahnke didn't meet Dayne until the team banquet following the 1999 season, but the running back quickly figured out who he was talking to. "He gave me a big smile," says Mahnke, who had become a local mini-celebrity of his own.

The Great Danes

Former Badger running back Ron Dayne was a man of relatively few words when it came to talking with the media during his days at Wisconsin. The man in charge of handling Dayne's media availabilities, then-sports information director Steve Malchow, decided to find something that might help tell Dayne's story without the running back having to do a lot of talking.

While visiting with Dayne one day, Malchow asked the Badger star if he had any pets as a child. Dayne told Malchow he loved dogs, and that, growing up, he had a dog named Butch. This prompted Malchow to ask Dayne if he would like to get involved in a public service campaign with the Dane County (Wisconsin) Humane Society.

"It seemed to make sense, playing off Ron's 'Great Dayne' nickname," Malchow recalled.

A photo shoot ensued as Dayne posed with four championship-level Great Danes. The image eventually wound up on a popular poster produced by the Dane County Humane Society. Dayne did radio and television public-service announcements on behalf of the organization, as well, supporting "the humane treatment of animals, not linebackers."

"The campaign ended up getting a lot of national publicity and won an award for the Dane County Humane Society," Malchow said. "It was a great cause, something Ron believed in, and I think it gave a little more substance to Ron's story."

Mike's Mettle

Mike Samuel quarterbacked the Badgers to 27 victories from 1996-1998. He left Wisconsin ranked third in school history in passing yardage (4,989), touchdowns (24) and completion percentage (.549). And he compiled those numbers while tailback Ron Dayne was busy rushing for the first 5,091 yards of his record-setting career. Samuel's career, however, was not defined by statistical accomplishments.

"The toughness he brought to the team was unbelievable," assistant coach Jim Hueber recalled years later. "His leadership qualities, the things other players told me after he left about how he handled himself and the team in the huddle, were probably things people didn't see, because he wasn't an outspoken guy."

Indeed, Samuel let his physical and mental toughness on the field do his talking for him. That was never more evident than during Wisconsin's 1997 home-opener against Boise State.

The Broncos, a 36-point underdog, came to Camp Randall Stadium on September 6 smarting from a 63-23 loss to Cal State-Northridge the week before. Boise State had surrendered a school-record 643 yards in the defeat. The program was, in fact, in just its second year as a Division IA competitor. But none of that seemed to matter once the Badgers and Broncos kicked off.

Dayne was out with an injury, and his replacement, Carl McCullough, fumbled on the first play of the game. Boise State's Jeff Davis returned it 33 yards for a touchdown. Samuel brought the Badgers back on the ensuing possession and scored on a one-yard run, but the Broncos held a 10-7 lead after the first quarter, thanks to a Todd Belcastro field goal that was set up by a Samuel interception.

Boise State intercepted Samuel a second time, and a short scoring drive produced a stunning 17-7 lead for the Broncos. McCullough, who rushed for 170 yards in the game, scored late in the first half to cut the deficit to 17-14. The Badgers then took a 21-17 lead into the fourth quarter, thanks to a seven-yard touchdown run by Cecil Martin early in the third frame.

Boise State, however, drove 73 yards in eight plays early in the fourth quarter to take a 24-21 lead. Each team then punted once before the Badgers got the ball back, only to lose it with 6:23 remaining when Samuel fumbled. But Wisconsin's defense held and the Badgers took over at their own 28-yard line with 4:10 remaining to play.

Samuel proceeded to guide the Badgers on a nine-play, 72-yard scoring drive that consumed 3:21 and ended with the Wisconsin quarterback running for a 12-yard touchdown on third-down and seven. Earlier in the drive, Samuel had rushed for 28 yards on third and 12 from the Wisconsin 47-yard line.

The Badgers had a 28-24 victory. Samuel, who had been replaced for a time during the game by Scott Kavanagh, had redeemed himself and earned the respect of his teammates. "He didn't give up and didn't let adversity or boos or anything get in the way of his heart and his spirit and what he wanted to do," Martin told the *Wisconsin State Journal* after the game. "When crunch time came, he stayed poised and focused."

"Money" Cashes in Twice

One of Wisconsin's most successful walk-on tales was about a guy they called "Money." Or, rather, he called himself "Money" and then so did everyone else.

Matt Davenport's reputation as one of the best kickers in Badger history is secure. He was a semifinalist for the Lou Groza Award as the nation's top kicker. He was a two-time consensus first-team All-Big Ten selection and left Wisconsin with the highest field goal percentage in school history. He began earning his reputation and his nickname during the 1997 season.

A transfer from Saddleback Junior College, Davenport was a walk-on backup to Badger senior starting kicker John Hall in 1996. As he attempted to earn the starting job for himself in 1997, Davenport told a reporter that he was "money from 45 yards in." He got a chance to prove his worth five games into the season.

The Badgers trailed a 1-3 Indiana squad, 26-24, with 10 seconds left to play and a Camp Randall Stadium crowd of 78,211 waiting to see if the five-foot-seven kicker from California could come through. He did. Davenport sailed a 43-yard field goal between the uprights and gave the Badgers a 27-26 win, causing head coach Barry Alvarez to state, "This is a rough way to make a living."

Davenport, however, cemented his place in Alvarez era history the following week at Northwestern. After the Badgers, who were trailing 25-23, had recovered a Wildcat fumble at the Wisconsin four-yard line with 1:16 left to play in the fourth quarter, they drove to the Northwestern 30-yard line.

Long snapper Mike Solwold, a freshman who had taken over for starter Mike Schneck (who was injured while celebrating Davenport's game-winning kick against Indiana a week earlier), had earlier in the game snapped a ball over punter Kevin Stemke's head. The error cost the Badgers a touchdown. Now, Solwold and Davenport had no room for error. Neither one made a mistake on this play.

Davenport launched a career-long 48-yard field goal that defeated the Wildcats with six seconds left to play. It turned out "Money" was good from outside 45 yards, too. Later that season he kicked a pair of field goals in Wisconsin's 13-10 upset win over

Matt Davenport, nicknamed "Money," was a two-time, first-team All-Big Ten selection.
Photo by David Stluka

12th-ranked Iowa, a victory that snapped the school's 18-game winless skid against the Hawkeyes.

An Inspiration to All

Cecil Martin had, on the surface, very little reason to feel or behave like the luckiest guy in the world. Yet that's just what he felt and behaved like during his five-year stint with the Badgers.

Martin's family struggled financially. He had seen the lives of many friends and acquaintances destroyed by drugs and crime. Martin and his mother, Diana, even spent time living in a homeless shelter after they lost their apartment the summer before his senior year in high school at Evanston (Illinois) Township.

But Martin's remarkably optimistic outlook and enthusiastic approach to everything helped him not only to endure, but to persevere and earn a scholarship to play for the Badgers.

"I had my hurdles and my family had tribulations to get over," Martin told the *Chicago Tribune* in 1995. "But I didn't have it nearly as bad as some kids."

Martin was a four-year starter as a fullback at Wisconsin. He was the lead blocker for the first three years of 1999 Heisman Trophy winner Ron Dayne's brilliant career. He rushed for 270 yards and added 431 receiving yards during his career. He also was a captain for the Badgers' 1998 Big Ten champion that went on to win the 1999 Rose Bowl.

Martin's legacy at Wisconsin, however, is as much off the field as on. A tireless volunteer, Martin established an off-season program with the UW Children's Hospital for players to visit hospitalized children. He was twice named to the American Football Coaches Association's "Good Works Team" for community service. He was recognizable all over campus for his infectious smile and enthusiasm for life and for the Badgers.

"Cecil was probably the most engaging young man I've ever been around or coached," said UW offensive coordinator and running backs coach Brian White. "When the Shoe Box and all the suspensions hit [prior to the 2000 season-opener against Western

Iowa, a victory that snapped the school's 18-game
against the Hawkeyes.

An Inspiration to All

Martin had, on the surface, very little reason to feel or
the luckiest guy in the world. Yet that's just what he felt
like during his five-year stint with the Badgers.

's family struggled financially. He had seen the lives of
ds and acquaintances destroyed by drugs and crime.
his mother, Diana, even spent time living in a homeless
they lost their apartment the summer before his senior
school at Evanston (Illinois) Township.

artin's remarkably optimistic outlook and enthusiastic
everything helped him not only to endure, but to
d earn a scholarship to play for the Badgers.

my hurdles and my family had tribulations to get over,"
the *Chicago Tribune* in 1995. "But I didn't have it nearly
me kids."

was a four-year starter as a fullback at Wisconsin. He
d blocker for the first three years of 1999 Heisman
her Ron Dayne's brilliant career. He rushed for 270 yards
431 receiving yards during his career. He also was a
he Badgers' 1998 Big Ten champion that went on to win
se Bowl.

's legacy at Wisconsin, however, is as much off the field
less volunteer, Martin established an off-season program
W Children's Hospital for players to visit hospitalized
e was twice named to the American Football Coaches
"Good Works Team" for community service. He was
all over campus for his infectious smile and enthusiasm
for the Badgers.

was probably the most engaging young man I've ever
d or coached," said UW offensive coordinator and
ks coach Brian White. "When the Shoe Box and all the
hit [prior to the 2000 season-opener against Western

"The toughness he brought to the team was unbelievable,"
assistant coach Jim Hueber recalled years later. "His leadership
qualities, the things other players told me after he left about how he
handled himself and the team in the huddle, were probably things
people didn't see, because he wasn't an outspoken guy."

Indeed, Samuel let his physical and mental toughness on the
field do his talking for him. That was never more evident than
during Wisconsin's 1997 home-opener against Boise State.

The Broncos, a 36-point underdog, came to Camp Randall
Stadium on September 6 smarting from a 63-23 loss to Cal State-
Northridge the week before. Boise State had surrendered a school-
record 643 yards in the defeat. The program was, in fact, in just its
second year as a Division IA competitor. But none of that seemed to
matter once the Badgers and Broncos kicked off.

Dayne was out with an injury, and his replacement, Carl
McCullough, fumbled on the first play of the game. Boise State's Jeff
Davis returned it 33 yards for a touchdown. Samuel brought the
Badgers back on the ensuing possession and scored on a one-yard
run, but the Broncos held a 10-7 lead after the first quarter, thanks
to a Todd Belcastro field goal that was set up by a Samuel
interception.

Boise State intercepted Samuel a second time, and a short
scoring drive produced a stunning 17-7 lead for the Broncos.
McCullough, who rushed for 170 yards in the game, scored late in
the first half to cut the deficit to 17-14. The Badgers then took a
21-17 lead into the fourth quarter, thanks to a seven-yard
touchdown run by Cecil Martin early in the third frame.

Boise State, however, drove 73 yards in eight plays early in the
fourth quarter to take a 24-21 lead. Each team then punted once
before the Badgers got the ball back, only to lose it with 6:23
remaining when Samuel fumbled. But Wisconsin's defense held and
the Badgers took over at their own 28-yard line with 4:10 remaining
to play.

Samuel proceeded to guide the Badgers on a nine-play, 72-yard
scoring drive that consumed 3:21 and ended with the Wisconsin
quarterback running for a 12-yard touchdown on third-down and
seven. Earlier in the drive, Samuel had rushed for 28 yards on third
and 12 from the Wisconsin 47-yard line.

The Badgers had a 28-24 victory. Samuel, who had been replaced for a time during the game by Scott Kavanagh, had redeemed himself and earned the respect of his teammates. "He didn't give up and didn't let adversity or boos or anything get in the way of his heart and his spirit and what he wanted to do," Martin told the *Wisconsin State Journal* after the game. "When crunch time came, he stayed poised and focused."

"Money" Cashes in Twice

One of Wisconsin's most successful walk-on tales was about a guy they called "Money." Or, rather, he called himself "Money" and then so did everyone else.

Matt Davenport's reputation as one of the best kickers in Badger history is secure. He was a semifinalist for the Lou Groza Award as the nation's top kicker. He was a two-time consensus first-team All-Big Ten selection and left Wisconsin with the highest field goal percentage in school history. He began earning his reputation and his nickname during the 1997 season.

A transfer from Saddleback Junior College, Davenport was a walk-on backup to Badger senior starting kicker John Hall in 1996. As he attempted to earn the starting job for himself in 1997, Davenport told a reporter that he was "money from 45 yards in." He got a chance to prove his worth five games into the season.

The Badgers trailed a 1-3 Indiana squad, 26-24, with 10 seconds left to play and a Camp Randall Stadium crowd of 78,211 waiting to see if the five-foot-seven kicker from California could come through. He did. Davenport sailed a 43-yard field goal between the uprights and gave the Badgers a 27-26 win, causing head coach Barry Alvarez to state, "This is a rough way to make a living."

Davenport, however, cemented his place in Alvarez era history the following week at Northwestern. After the Badgers, who were trailing 25-23, had recovered a Wildcat fumble at the Wisconsin four-yard line with 1:16 left to play in the fourth quarter, they drove to the Northwestern 30-yard line.

Long snapper Mike Solwo for starter Mike Schneck (w Davenport's game-winning kick earlier in the game snapped a ba The error cost the Badgers Davenport had no room for er this play.

Davenport launched a c defeated the Wildcats with six "Money" was good from outsid kicked a pair of field goals in

Matt Davenport, nicknamed "Money," wa
Photo by David Stluka

12th-ranke winless ski

Cecil behave like and behave

Marti many frier Martin and shelter afte year in hig

But N approach persevere a

"I had Martin tol as bad as s

Marti was the le Trophy wir and added captain for the 1999 F

Marti as on. A ti with the U children. F Association recognizab for life and

"Ceci been arou running ba suspension

Fullback Cecil Martin *Photo by David Stluka*

Michigan], I remember getting a call from Cecil. The story had already hit the wires and he had my cell phone number and he called me about two hours before the game and wanted to talk to some of the players, and he did and it was pretty inspiring stuff. He is very aware of when things are tough. That's when you get a call from Cecil."

Martin went on to play five years in the National Football League for the Philadelphia Eagles and Tampa Bay Buccaneers. He earned the 2000 Ed Block Courage Award, which goes to NFL players who exemplify commitment to the principles of sportsmanship and courage.

California Dreamin'

When head coach Barry Alvarez called his football team together for a meeting early in the spring semester of 1998, he spoke to a group that had a few weeks earlier been handed a one-sided, 33-6 defeat by Georgia in the 1998 Outback Bowl.

As Alvarez neared the end of his address to players and coaches about where the program was and what its goals would be in the coming weeks and months, he asked if anyone in the McClain Auditorium had anything to say.

Still just a sophomore, offensive tackle Chris McIntosh rose from his seat, walked to the front of the room and pronounced, "I didn't come here to go to the Outback Bowl. I came here to win the Big Ten championship and play in the Rose Bowl."

Assistant coach Brian White remembers sitting in the back of the room with other staff members and wondering if he really heard what he had just heard.

"I'm sitting in the back thinking that it'd be one thing if we'd just beaten a good Georgia team, but that was the last thing I expected to hear," White said.

McIntosh, however, had vaulted himself into a leadership role within the program. He was joined the following season by linebackers Donnel Thompson and Bob Adamov, and fullback Cecil Martin to form one of the strongest groups of team captains of the Alvarez era.

McIntosh ended up starting a school-record 50 games in his career, including victories over UCLA and Stanford in the 1999 and 2000 Rose Bowls, respectively.

The Breaks of the Game

Starting 50 consecutive football games during a four-year career requires, among other things, getting a good break once in a while. That's just what Chris McIntosh got in the Badgers' 1998 season opener.

Wisconsin traveled West to begin its 1998 campaign at night against San Diego State. The Badgers were facing adversity right off the bat, because star running back Ron Dayne would miss the game with a sprained ankle, and backup Eddie Faulkner left the game in the first quarter with a shoulder injury.

The Aztecs and 20th-ranked Badgers proceeded to battle to a 7-7 tie at halftime, as both offenses struggled to find their rhythm. McIntosh almost joined the wounded on the sidelines during a second-quarter series.

"I was cutting a guy, and I think I got it caught in the ground," McIntosh said of his right thumb in an interview with *The Capital Times*. "I came off, they determined it was busted, and they put a cast on it at halftime."

McIntosh, however, was determined to keep playing. It would be an understatement to say he scoffed at the doctor's suggestion that he not return to the game. "I think I kind of scared our doctor when he told me I had to come out," McIntosh told the *Wisconsin State Journal.*

McIntosh's brand of toughness and fortitude was emblematic of the Badgers' 26-14 victory that night. Wisconsin trailed 14-13 early in the fourth quarter, but Mike Samuel turned a quarterback draw into a 47-yard touchdown run with 11:56 remaining to play. The Badger defense stymied the Aztecs the rest of the way, and Wisconsin was on its way to what became the winningest season in school history.

Gibby

John Dettmann vividly remembers the first time he saw Aaron Gibson in person. The Badgers were holding a recruiting meal at the Union South on the UW-Madison campus.

"I could see this body coming down the hallway with his parents, but I couldn't really see him," says Dettmann, the Badgers' strength and conditioning coach. "Then he walked through the door [a normal single door frame] and he actually had to turn sideways to walk through it. I had never seen a person who had to tilt their shoulders like that to get through a door."

It's probably safe to say Dettmann was not the only one on campus who had never met someone as large as Gibson. The offensive tackle from Indianapolis was six foot seven, 378 pounds, with size 19 shoes and a size 62 jacket. His waist was 47 and one-half inches around. The helmet he wore at Wisconsin was the largest that equipment maker Riddell had ever produced. There was, however, more to Gibson than just his physical stature.

"He was one of the kindest athletes I ever got a chance to work with," said then sports information director Steve Malchow. "He had a very good sense of humor. It hit me when I traveled with him on the awards circuit. It was ridiculous how many times he got asked, 'How big are you?' Yet never once did I see him lose his patience with that. He just kind of laughed and responded nicely. He was really easygoing."

Gibson, whose remarkable athletic skills enabled him to do the splits as well as dunk a basketball, also wrote poetry and enjoyed fishing. But it was his size, strength and playing ability that drew national attention.

Gibson started his career at Wisconsin as a blocking tight end (he would wear number 81) in 1996. The following season, a year in which he was featured in a *New York Times Magazine* article as well as ABC News's *20/20*, Gibson started 10 games at right tackle and three more as a third tight end.

By the start of his senior year in 1998, Gibson was in perhaps the best shape of his life, and his performance on the field bore that out. He earned consensus All-America honors and was a finalist for both the Lombardi Award and Outland Trophy as he helped the Badgers to the Big Ten title by opening holes for All-America running back Ron Dayne.

Gibson went on to play in the National Football League after the Detroit Lions selected him in the first round (27th overall) of the 1999 NFL Draft.

Tale of the Tape

John Dettmann, the Badger football program's strength and conditioning coach, once decided to try on mammoth offensive tackle Aaron Gibson's sideline coat. It was a XXXXXL.

"I put the coat on and it went all the way to the floor," Dettmann recalled. "It was like a sleeping bag for me. Then I had

Offensive tackle Aaron Gibson *Photo by David Stluka*

him take off his shoes. I put my feet inside his shoes with my shoes (size 11) still on. They fit!"

Here is the tale of the tape for Gibson, touted as the largest player in Wisconsin football history:

Height: six foot seven
Weight: 378 lbs.
Neck: 20 ½ inches
Chest (expanded): 58 ¾ inches
Reach: 87 inches (40 ½ inch sleeves)
Bicep: 20 ¼ inches
Waist: 47 ½ inches
Thigh: 33 ½ inches
Shoe size: 19
Jacket size: 62

Badgers Brees by Purdue

Purdue broke the records and gained the yards. All Wisconsin got out of its 1998 game with the Boilermakers was a victory.

The Badgers, ranked 10th nationally in the coaches poll, were 5-0 overall and 2-0 in the Big Ten heading into their October 10 Homecoming game with Purdue. It was just the third night game in Camp Randall Stadium history, and the Badgers had lost both of the previous two. Wisconsin also brought the nation's No. 3 scoring and No. 5 total defense into the contest against the pass-happy Purdue offense directed by sophomore quarterback Drew Brees.

The Boilermakers (3-2 overall and 1-0 in conference play) entered the game averaging 317.2 passing yards per game (seventh in the nation), but no one could have predicted the kind of aerial assault they would throw at the Badgers that night.

Wisconsin took a 14-3 lead after the first quarter, thanks to touchdown runs of nine and 16 yards by quarterback Mike Samuel. The Badgers had controlled Brees, allowing him to complete eight of 14 passes with an interception. They had no idea, however, that he would average 23 passing attempts *per quarter* the rest of the game.

Purdue's Travis Dorsch sandwiched second-quarter field goals of 44 and 45 yards around a 25-yard field goal by Wisconsin's Matt Davenport and a six-yard touchdown pass from Brees to Chris Daniels, and the teams went to halftime tied 17-17. Brees had completed 24 of 36 passes for 206 yards by the midway point of the game.

The Boilermakers opened the second half by marching 70 yards to the Wisconsin 10-yard line where they faced third-down and four. Brees was a remarkable eight-for-10 passing on the drive up to that point, but his 11th attempt was intercepted by Badger freshman cornerback Mike Echols. It would not be the last pick of the night by a Wisconsin rookie defensive back.

Later in the third quarter a penalty and a quarterback sack forced Wisconsin's Kevin Stemke to punt from his own 20-yard line. Purdue's Da'Shann Austin returned it to the Purdue 45-yard line. The Boilermakers rushed for two yards on their first play before Jamar Fletcher, another of the Badgers' freshman cornerbacks, stepped up, intercepted a Brees pass and returned it 52 yards for a touchdown.

After Wisconsin stopped Purdue on fourth down and one early in the fourth quarter, tailback Ron Dayne culminated a nearly six-minute drive with a one-yard touchdown run for a 31-17 lead. Purdue's ensuing possession ended in a Bobby Myers interception in the end zone. The Boilermakers added a late touchdown, but Wisconsin's Chris Chambers recovered Purdue's onside kick with 21 seconds left to play to ensure the win.

"I don't think I'll have to answer any more questions about whether our young secondary has been tested," Alvarez said after the game. "They had a lifetime of tests today."

Brees set an NCAA record with 83 passing attempts and tied an NCAA mark with 55 completions. He threw for 494 yards but also was intercepted four times. Purdue's Randall Lane set the Big Ten record with 18 receptions.

An interesting footnote is that during the game the toilets on the east side of the stadium failed and had to be shut down. That led, in part, to discussions that eventually resulted in the massive Camp Randall Stadium renovation of the early part of the 21st century.

Jump Around!

Wisconsin's 31-24 victory over Purdue on October 10, 1998, is memorable mostly for Boilermaker quarterback Drew Brees's NCAA-record 83 passing attempts (and NCAA record-tying 55 completions) and freshman Jamar Fletcher's 52-yard interception return for a touchdown in the third quarter that provided the winning margin.

The game is memorable, however, for another reason: it was the beginning of "Jump Around."

Kevin Kluender was in his second year as an assistant marketing director at Wisconsin that fall. Kluender's job at Badger home games was to cue up music and to work in conjunction with public address man Mike Mahnke.

That season marked the debut of the "student section race," a mock competition run on the stadium scoreboard in which the letters representing the student sections at Camp Randall Stadium (K, L, M, N, O and P) raced against each other. The race, always run at the end of the third quarter, was usually followed by music that Kluender selected.

Ryan Sondrup, a former Badger football player and then volunteer in the athletic marketing office, had (along with some other Badgers) come up with a list of contemporary music to be played in the stadium during games. That evening Kluender chose "Jump Around," a song released in 1992 by a group called House of Pain.

"I remember thinking maybe the students would get into it," Kluender recalled. "I initially turned my back to the field while the song was playing, but I saw people in the press box pointing out to the field. I turned back around and it looked like popcorn popping."

Indeed, the student section (which included Sondrup that night) had embraced the song by doing just what it said: jumping around. Since that game against Purdue, fans all over the stadium have taken to jumping to the hip-hop tune.

Kluender, however, is not completely comfortable with taking credit for introducing "Jump Around" to Camp Randall Stadium.

"The song was already in our computer when I got to Wisconsin," Kluender said. "I'm sure it had been played before. But that Purdue game was the first time we did it in the format that we've maintained over the years."

Nick Was Quick

The story seemed to have become legend in less time than it took Nick Davis to run a punt back 82 yards for a touchdown in Wisconsin's 1998 Big Ten title-clinching 24-3 victory over Penn State.

Head coach Barry Alvarez, aware that his team had finished last in the Big Ten in punt returns in 1997, approached Davis and asked the true freshman if he could catch punts. Davis responded by saying, "I could catch a BB in the dark if I had to."

The confident rookie then went out and backed up his statement by leading the Big Ten with a 15.3-yard punt-return average. He brought back two punts for touchdowns, including the electrifying return against the Nittany Lions.

Davis, a native of tiny Manchester, Michigan, who played two seasons with the Minnesota Vikings, ended his career with the Badgers as one of just nine players in NCAA history with 1,000 career yards on both punt and kickoff returns. He scored five career touchdowns on returns (three punt and two kickoff).

A Close Shave

Assistant coach Brian White found out in the fall of 1998 that the running backs he was coaching had pretty good memories.

Tailback Eddie Faulkner had shaved the heads of the Badger running backs during training camp and White complimented the group on how good they looked. Faulkner offered White the same service. The coach politely declined, but told Faulkner that if the Badgers were 9-0 heading into their game at Michigan on November 14, then he would allow his head to be shaved.

Later that fall, as the unbeaten (8-0) and eighth-ranked Badgers were preparing to host Minnesota, White was conducting a Tuesday meeting when Faulkner spoke up.

"Hey Coach White, you know you are going to be bald after Saturday's game," Faulkner asserted. White's response? "What are you talking about?" The players then reminded White about his early-season promise. To his credit, White told the players that if they defeated the Golden Gophers, they could, indeed, shave his head.

The Badgers used a suffocating defense and terrific special teams play to key a 26-7 victory over Minnesota. "I didn't take three steps before [offensive linemen] Chris McIntosh and Casey Rabach grabbed me and carried me into the locker room," White said. "Some other players already had the razor ready, and they all took turns scalping my head."

White, a quarterback at Harvard in the 1980s, had also had his head shaved as an assistant coach at Nevada in 1993.

"Those Harvard graduates do some silly things," Badger head coach Barry Alvarez said after the game.

Wendell Comes of Age

Wendell Bryant was a two-time Big Ten Defensive Lineman of the Year and a first-team All-American in 2001, but many Badger fans remember him for a key play he made as a true freshman in the 1999 Rose Bowl.

The Badgers had outscored UCLA, 38-31, and punted to the Bruins, who took over at their own 46-yard line with 1:42 remaining to play in the game. UCLA quarterback Cade McNown sandwiched two incomplete passes around a seven-yard completion that left the

Bruins with a fourth-and-three situation at the Wisconsin 47-yard line.

Bryant proceeded to live out the dream of any college football player. He sacked McNown to end the Bruins' hopes and secure Wisconsin's second Rose Bowl victory in five years.

"It was crunch time," Bryant recalled. "We realized that if they scored, they could win. Basically I just tried to block everything out and just go. McNown never saw me coming. I realized when I stood up that it was over."

The play capped a terrific year for Bryant, who was overjoyed just to be winning.

"For me it had already been a phenomenal year," Bryant said. "My high school team hadn't been very successful so, for me, being on a team that was 10-1 and had won the Big Ten championship, I was already happy. Being around the leaders we had on that team was a great experience for me. Playing in the Rose Bowl was just icing on the cake."

A Diamond in the Rough

It's strange how things work out sometimes. The quarterback with the most wins in Wisconsin history and who led the school to a Big Ten and Rose Bowl title as a redshirt freshman may never have become a Badger were it not for his mother's willingness to drive through the night from Fargo, North Dakota, to Madison, Wisconsin, so her son could attend football camp.

Brooks Bollinger, whose father, Rob, was offensive coordinator for the University of North Dakota's football team, was a star athlete regardless the sport. But he was being recruited, albeit lightly, by Wisconsin, Iowa, Minnesota, Wyoming, and some Division II schools. Bollinger had attended football camp at Iowa and had decided to attend the camp at Wisconsin, too.

"I was playing baseball in Bismarck," Bollinger recalled. "We drove back to Fargo where I met my mom and we started to drive to Madison around 11:00 p.m. My mom doesn't like to drive at night and then we had to drive through a terrible rainstorm."

Bollinger and his mother got to Madison at around 7:00 a.m. Brooks met with the Badger coaches that morning, worked out at the camp for a day and a half and was offered a scholarship.

"I knew nothing about Madison or Wisconsin at the time," Bollinger said. "I probably didn't even evaluate it as closely as I should have. But I had enjoyed it, and figured I would get a good education, so I accepted."

Bollinger went on to quarterback the Badgers to 30 wins during his career. He left Wisconsin as one of seven quarterbacks in Big Ten history with 30 wins and as one of seven players in Big Ten annals with at least 20 rushing and 30 passing touchdowns.

A Memorable Day at "The Horseshoe"

Ohio Stadium would not top any list of places that a visiting football team would like to play in to end a two-game losing streak with a redshirt freshman quarterback making his first career start. That is, however, what faced Wisconsin on October 2, 1999.

The Badgers were the defending Big Ten champions, but had lost back-to-back games at Cincinnati and at home against Michigan. They had fallen from the top 25, and their starting quarterback, Scott Kavanaugh, was banged up. They were playing a 12th-ranked Ohio State team in a facility in which only two Wisconsin teams had ever won.

It would be an understatement to say things did not start well for the Badgers. Wisconsin lost a fumble on the third play of the game and was forced to punt on its next three possessions as Ohio State built a 17-0 lead before the game was 20 minutes old.

Late in the first half, however, the Badgers showed some life by converting scoring drives of 47 and 78 yards, respectively, into a pair of Vitaly Pisetsky field goals.

Ohio State's Michael Wiley then fumbled the second-half kickoff. Wisconsin's Bobby Myers recovered the ball and tailback Ron Dayne scored two plays later. The momentum had changed. The Badgers, led by quarterback Brooks Bollinger and the Heisman Trophy-bound Dayne, scored four touchdowns and a field goal on

Brooks Bollinger became the winningest quarterback in school history.
Photo by David Stluka

their next five possessions and shut out the Buckeyes in the second half for a remarkable 42-17 victory.

Bollinger completed 15 of 27 passes for 167 yards and no interceptions. Dayne carried 32 times for 161 yards and four scores. And the Badger defense limited Ohio State to just 113 yards in the second half.

"That was a good, old-fashioned butt kicking," Ohio State head coach John Cooper said afterward. "You have to give Wisconsin credit."

The significance of the greatest comeback win of the Alvarez era to that point in time was not lost on director of athletics Pat Richter, who asked Alvarez if he could address the team after the game.

"I get misty-eyed thinking about it," Richter recalled more than five years later. "I never wanted to get myself into Barry's business, but I just felt like I wanted to say something, seeing how proud people were about what had happened, so I asked Barry if he'd mind if I talked to the team. As a former player, you know the gratification they felt, and I just wanted the team to know how good people felt about what they had done."

A Group Effort

Wisconsin's win at Minnesota in 1999 was noteworthy not only because it was the first overtime game in school history, but also because it was the only game of the Barry Alvarez era that the Badger head coach did not attend.

Alvarez had injured his knee prior to the first game of the season but was also fighting an infection. He had started taking the field in a golf cart.

"I was in so much pain after the Cincinnati game [on September 18] that Pat [Richter] said to me, 'That's it, you're going to Mayo,'" Alvarez recalled. Alvarez went to the Mayo Clinic in Rochester, Minnesota, where arrangements were made for him to have a knee operation the week of the Badgers' game at Minnesota.

(Doctors operated but, due to the infection, were unable to replace Alvarez's knee until after the season).

Wisconsin traveled to Minnesota for an October 9 matchup with the 25th-ranked Golden Gophers. The Badgers were fresh off their 42-17 victory at 12th-rated Ohio State and were looking to become the first team in school history to win back-to-back road games against nationally ranked opponents. They were, however, going to have to do it without their head coach.

The night before the game the Badgers watched Alvarez speak to them on a message he had videotaped earlier from his hospital bed. Assistant head coach John Palermo assumed the Wisconsin head coaching duties that week.

"Probably the biggest difference for me was being there at the game without him there and having to make some bigger decisions than I maybe had been faced with before," Palermo recalled.

Chadima was connected to Alvarez via phone the entire game and passed it along to whomever Alvarez wanted to speak with.

The game itself was a dogfight. The two teams battled to a 14-14 halftime tie and then to a 17-17 deadlock at the end of regulation thanks to a 36-yard Vitaly Pisetsky field goal with 2:59 remaining to play in the fourth quarter.

The Badgers won the overtime coin toss and elected to go on defense. Minnesota, however, backed itself up into a fourth down-and-30 situation. Wisconsin All-America cornerback Jamar Fletcher ended the Golden Gophers' hopes with a fourth-down interception. Wisconsin then drove to the Minnesota 13-yard line, and Pisetsky booted the game-winning, 31-yard field goal.

"I was screaming and yelling in there and people are coming down the hall telling me to quiet down," Alvarez recalled of his afternoon watching from the hospital. "It was really difficult, but you do what you have to do."

The Golden Gophers kept Badger tailback Ron Dayne in check, holding him to just 80 yards on 25 carries. But redshirt freshman quarterback Brooks Bollinger followed his first career start (at Ohio State the week before) with another fine performance. Bollinger rushed for 62 yards, while completing 11 of 21 passes for

212 yards and a touchdown. The Badger defense limited Minnesota to 132 yards and three points after halftime.

It was an emotional scene in the Badger locker room afterward as coaches and players spoke to Alvarez over the phone. "It was really emotional for all of our coaches, because it wasn't one guy doing it all," Palermo said. "Everyone sort of came together and got it done."

Tauscher's Remarkable Journey

There have been a number of walk-on success stories during the Barry Alvarez era at Wisconsin, but few have taken as many odd twists and turns as Mark Tauscher's.

Tauscher, a native of Auburndale, Wisconsin, joined the Badgers as a non-scholarship player and eventually earned his first letter as a backup offensive tackle in 1998. Tauscher, a reserve left tackle, played occasionally at right tackle when the Badgers slid starting right tackle Aaron Gibson to the left side of the line to form a tandem with left tackle Chris McIntosh.

Once the 1998 season (and, he figured, his career) was over, Tauscher looked toward earning his degree in May of 1999, while making time to travel to both the Super Bowl and Kentucky Derby. After graduation, he had planned to find a job, but changed his mind and appeared headed to Youngstown State to play football and continue his education. That's when the Wisconsin coaching staff discovered he had one more year of eligibility left.

"Quite frankly, I didn't realize he had a fifth year," head coach Barry Alvarez told *The Capital Times* in 1999.

Convinced to return to the Badgers, Tauscher gained admission to the UW's graduate school. He joined the team at fall camp and took over the right tackle spot. Tauscher ended up starting all 12 games as the Badgers led the Big Ten in rushing. He was the only Badger to play in two postseason all-star games in January of 2000, traveling to both the Hula Bowl and East-West Shrine Game.

Tauscher's story, however, did not end there. The former walk-on who almost quit playing football was selected by his home-state Green Bay Packers in the seventh round of the 2000 National Football League draft. He has started for the Packers since 2000.

Offensive tackle Mark Tauscher *Photo by David Stluka*

Dayne Demolishes Michigan State

It was, quite frankly, shocking. There was no other word to describe the way Wisconsin's running game trampled Michigan State's No. 1-ranked rushing defense on a cool, October day at Camp Randall Stadium in 1999.

The 17th-ranked Badgers had won two straight games, but were coming home to face what was expected to be a very stiff test. Eleventh-ranked Michigan State, owner of the nation's top-rated run defense, was allowing a mere 39.9 yards per game on the ground. That average, however, went up in a hurry.

Wisconsin, which forced a punt on Michigan State's game-opening possession, went 87 yards in just four plays to take a 7-0 lead before anyone knew what happened. Tailback Ron Dayne gained 72 yards on the drive that ended with his 51-yard touchdown run.

"The first series they had four plays and however many yards they had," Michigan State head coach Nick Saban said after the game. "That was a little bit shocking to me, because I thought we were ready to play."

Dayne wound up gaining 214 of the Badgers' 301 rushing yards that day against a Spartan run defense whose "worst" performance of the season before meeting the Badgers was a 108-yard effort by Notre Dame.

"Fletch" Backs It Up

In his role as sports information director at the University of Wisconsin, Steve Malchow's job sometimes required him to counsel or advise Badger football players on how to respond to questions from the media. He generally had minimal concern that a player might say something that would be considered "bulletin-board material." There was, however, at least one exception.

"I was always nervous that Jamar Fletcher would say something that might be misconstrued," Malchow recalled of Fletcher, one of the most self-confident players of the Barry Alvarez era. "But he loved to lay a challenge out there and then meet the challenge. He was one of the best playmakers we ever had here."

One of Fletcher's greatest performances came on the heels of one of his most confident public statements. The Badgers were beginning preparations for a showdown with 11th-ranked Michigan State at Camp Randall Stadium on October 23, 1999. In addition to their top-ranked run defense, the Spartans featured Plaxico Burress, a six-foot-six receiver regarded as one of the Big Ten's best.

Fletcher told reporters on the Monday before the game that he wanted to cover Burress and would demand to do so if necessary. Fortunately for the Badgers, Fletcher did cover Burress. While running back Ron Dayne was busy rushing for 214 yards and two touchdowns, Fletcher was intercepting two passes and helping to limit Burress to an inconsequential five receptions for 58 yards.

"I've got one saying and I stole it from Lou Holtz," Alvarez said after the Badgers' 40-10 victory. "If your mouth writes a check, your fanny better be able to cash it."

Cornerback Jamar Fletcher regularly shut down opposing receivers. *Photo by David Stluka*

Barry Becomes Wins King

It wasn't exactly lost in the shuffle, but head coach Barry Alvarez's 66th victory at Wisconsin was not the focal point of the Badgers' 40-10 rout of 11th-ranked Michigan State in 1999. And that's just the way the coach wanted it.

The win allowed Alvarez to become Wisconsin's career leader in coaching victories, eclipsing Phil King (1896-1902, 1905) on the school's all-time list. His mind, however, was elsewhere after the game.

"Right now I'm more concerned with this win and where our kids are for the stretch run," Alvarez said. "I think someday I'll look back and relish the victories we've had and remember all the great kids who played for us and the great staffs of coaches that coached for me. But right now it really doesn't mean a whole lot. I'm more concerned with this football team and where we're going this season."

The Perfect Day

Former Wisconsin director of athletics Pat Richter said it was like theater. That may be, but what scriptwriter could possibly have dreamed up the chain of events that took place in Camp Randall Stadium on an unseasonably warm November afternoon in 1999?

Everyone—coaches, players, fans, media—knew what was at stake as the ninth-ranked Badgers prepared all week to host Iowa. A Michigan victory over Penn State, combined with a Wisconsin win over the Hawkeyes, would give the Badgers their second straight Big Ten title (this time undisputed) and send them back to the Rose Bowl. In addition, tailback Ron Dayne, his drive to the Heisman Trophy continuing to gain momentum, needed just 99 yards to become the NCAA Division I-A career rushing leader. The sense of anticipation in Madison that week was undeniable.

"Coming in [toward the stadium] on the bus, you could feel the excitement," assistant coach Jeff Horton recalled. "It was just different coming in. You could tell it was cranked up even more than normal. People were on the streets and were well into their partying. When we stepped off the bus, there was a big crowd there to see us."

The game was set for a 2:30 p.m. start. ABC was in town to televise the game, and the contest began with a clear sky and 67-degree weather at kickoff.

The Badgers had not even scored yet when the first cheer of the day swept through the crowd of 79,404. Early in the first quarter it was announced that Michigan had upset Penn State, giving the Badgers the chance to win the league title outright.

Wisconsin struggled to move the ball on its first possession of the game but moved out to a 13-0 first-quarter lead after scoring drives of 80 and 73 yards. Iowa opened the second-quarter scoring with a field goal before quarterback Brooks Bollinger hit Chris Chambers with a 24-yard touchdown pass for a 20-3 Wisconsin lead. Next up was the record.

Dayne had rushed for 76 yards when Wisconsin took possession of the ball with 4:40 remaining in the first half. On first-and-10 from the Wisconsin 17-yard line, the Badgers called a 23 Zone play, and 31 yards later Dayne had bypassed the career rushing record that had been set by Texas's Ricky Williams just a year earlier.

"[Fullback] Chad Kuhns told me, 'You can't do it without me.'" Dayne said after the game. "We ran 23-something, we got a couple names for it. When I broke out and then got up, Chad and everybody was around me."

Fans at the game that day will also recall a streaker who raced the length of the field during the stoppage that immediately followed Dayne's record run.

All that remained was finishing off the Hawkeyes, and the Badgers did that by scoring once more in the first half for a 27-3 lead at the break before adding a pair of touchdowns in the second half. Dayne rushed for 216 yards on 27 carries. Bollinger, who later called the game "the best football atmosphere I've ever been around," added 113 rushing yards and a touchdown to go along with 9-for-12 passing for 144 yards and three touchdowns. Wisconsin limited Iowa to just 247 yards in total offense.

As the clocked ticked down, head coach Barry Alvarez, who had spent much of the season watching games from press boxes due to knee problems, made his way to the field on crutches. Alvarez and Dayne found each other on the Badger sideline and embraced.

"I'll never forget that big smile of his," Alvarez said after the game. "When you go down to the sideline and see him smiling and trying to work his way over to me, you'll always have that picture in your mind."

The postgame festivities may have been more memorable than the game itself. Darkness had fallen over Madison, and on the field the Badgers were accepting the Big Ten championship trophy, as well as an invitation to the Rose Bowl. But that was not all.

Steve Malchow, then the Wisconsin sports information director, grabbed Dayne, looked him in the eye and told him his name and number were about to be unveiled on the façade of the stadium. "I told him I couldn't write a speech for him," Malchow recalled. He did not have to.

"I just want to say to all the fans, thanks, I love you all," Dayne said to the crowd, which spontaneously responded by holding up white towels [with a red number 33 printed on them] that had been distributed before the game. It was a remarkable sight and a fitting end to a perfect afternoon.

The Speech

College football fans know that the final piece to the Heisman Trophy presentation in New York City is the winner's acceptance speech. Former Wisconsin sports information director Steve Malchow knew that and made sure running back Ron Dayne knew it, too.

"Most people know Ron was a quiet guy, but I told him before we left Madison that he would need to write a speech," Malchow recalled. "He said he would."

Dayne took a swing at it with the assistance of a few staff members, but Malchow felt the language did not sound like Dayne. "I told him I felt the speech should be simple: thank the Downtown Athletic Club and thank the people that have meant something to you," Malchow said.

Ron Dayne (33) became college football's career rushing leader with his performance against Iowa in 1999. *Photo by David Stluka*

Dayne and Malchow had traveled to Orlando, Florida, for ESPN's *College Football Awards Show* on the way to New York City. Malchow had seen no evidence of Dayne's speech, and he began to grow nervous and frustrated. Then his hotel room phone rang. Dayne wanted him to come down to his room.

"I walked into his room and he said, 'I want to give you my speech,'" Malchow recalled. "He did and it was one of the best speeches I had ever heard. It was genuine and it was so 'him.' I was proud of him because I saw that he understood the magnitude of what he was going through and I felt like I had reached him."

Dayne Meets a Potential President

The path traveled by a Heisman Trophy winner inevitably extends beyond just the world of sports.

"We were waiting to go up in an elevator after Ron Dayne had won the Heisman Trophy in New York," recalled then Wisconsin director of athletics Pat Richter. "I asked Ron if he wanted to meet a presidential candidate, and he said yes."

Richter and Dayne then proceeded to introduce themselves to Bill Bradley, the former Princeton and New York Knicks great, who was at the time trying to become the Democratic presidential nominee.

A Not-So-Secret Weapon

In sports terminology, the word "weapon" is often associated with someone capable of producing offensively. It's a scorer in basketball, a skill position player in football, or a dangerous hitter in baseball.

Punters are not really thought of as "weapons" but that is precisely what Kevin Stemke was during his four seasons (1997-2000) at Wisconsin. The left-footed Stemke consistently contributed to and, sometimes, controlled Wisconsin's ability to dictate games with field position. The Badgers were 38-12, including two Big Ten and Rose Bowl championships, during Stemke's career.

The Green Bay, Wisconsin, native had played soccer his entire life before going out for football as a high school freshman. He ended up as a four-year varsity letterwinner.

Stemke's 43.9-yard punting average at Wisconsin in 1997 was a school freshman record and was second in the Big Ten. It also earned him second-team All-Big Ten honors. Remarkably consistent, Stemke followed his rookie year by leading the conference as a sophomore with a 43.8-yard average. His average dipped to 41.3 as a junior, but the best was yet to come.

Stemke earned first-team All-America honors and won the inaugural Ray Guy Award as the nation's top punter in 2000. He finished third nationally with a 44.5-yard average and was a consensus first-team All-Big Ten selection.

Wisconsin's career record-holder for punting yards (10,660), Stemke also set the school standard for punting average (43.5), which was fourth in Big Ten history when he left Madison.

CHAPTER ELEVEN

2000-2004

Wisconsin went to bowl games in four of the new century's first five seasons and won nine games twice, including 2000 and 2004. The 2004 team began its season with a 9-0 mark before finishing 9-3 with an appearance in the Outback Bowl. The period also witnessed the $109 million renovation of Camp Randall Stadium.

Hero on a Hot Summer Night

Josh Hunt woke up on the morning of August 31, 2000, having never returned a punt in a game during his three-year career as a Badger. Twenty-four hours later he was a hero.

Hunt, a walk-on from Thiensville, Wisconsin, had joined the Wisconsin football program in 1997. His greatest claim to fame during his first three seasons was being named the team's scout team player of the week for his performance in helping prepare the Badgers' starters to play Boise State in 1997. That all changed, however, on a muggy, late-summer evening in Madison.

Wisconsin's hopes for the 2000 season were understandably high. The program was coming off back-to-back Big Ten and Rose Bowl titles and returned 16 starters. The Associated Press tabbed the Badgers fourth nationally in its preseason poll. Fans dreamt not of a return trip to the Rose Bowl, but rather an appearance in the Orange Bowl, site of the Bowl Championship Series national championship game that season.

But the hopes of Badger fans, coaches and players were dealt a severe blow before the season ever got started. Just hours before Wisconsin was to open the season at home against Western Michigan, it was revealed that 11 Badgers would have to serve suspensions that night in response to the NCAA's determination that a number of Badger student-athletes had received extra benefits. One of the suspended players was star punt return specialist Nick Davis.

Coach Barry Alvarez and his staff scrambled to patch together a lineup that included eight first-time starters. It also featured an unknown walk-on with no name on his jersey as the punt returner.

A first-quarter field goal by Wisconsin's Vitaly Pisetsky had accounted for the game's only scoring as the second-quarter clock ticked toward halftime. The Badgers' offense wasn't having much luck, but their defense was as stifling as the 90-degree heat. As the Broncos' Matt Steffen prepared to punt from his own 32-yard line, Hunt lined up to field the ball some 50 yards away.

Hunt took Steffen's 57-yard punt at the 11-yard line, evaded a couple Bronco defenders, got a block from fellow receiver Lee Evans, and was gone. His 89-yard return for a touchdown was the second-longest in school history and ended up providing the Badgers with the deciding points in their 19-7 victory.

"I just found out today [that he would be playing], a few hours before the game," Hunt said after the win. "I catch punts in practice all the time, and I was prepared. I told the coaches I could do that, and I just went out and did it."

Hunt returned six other punts that season for a total of just 34 yards.

Replacing Ron Dayne

The end of the Ron Dayne era at Wisconsin inevitably produced the question. How do you replace college football's career rushing leader and the 1999 Heisman Trophy winner? Junior Michael Bennett, as it turned out, had the answer.

Bennett had gained 298 yards as a backup tailback during his sophomore year (1999), including a 114-yard effort in a 59-0 rout of Indiana, so he was not exactly a novice. But he really put his stamp on the Badger football program with a signature game that would have made Dayne proud.

Wisconsin, ranked fifth in the nation, was still adjusting to NCAA-imposed player suspensions that resulted from the "Shoe Box" affair when unranked (and underrated) Oregon visited Camp Randall Stadium on September 9, 2000. The Badgers had won their opener, 19-7, over Western Michigan nine days earlier.

The Ducks kicked a pair of second-quarter field goals and limited Wisconsin to a paltry 45 yards in total offense on the way to a 6-0 halftime lead. Bennett was held to just 32 rushing yards on 11 carries, but he was, as it turns out, just getting warmed up.

Oregon kicked off to start the second half, and Bennett capped the Badgers' 80-yard scoring drive with a 59-yard touchdown run that gave the UW a 7-6 lead. Ryan Marks blocked an Oregon punt that gave Wisconsin a 14-6 advantage, before Bennett followed a Duck field goal with a 75-yard touchdown run that put the Badgers ahead, 20-9.

The visitors, however, would not go away. Oregon added a touchdown pass and an interception return for a touchdown that gave the Ducks a 23-20 lead with 6:09 remaining in the fourth quarter. But Bennett electrified the Camp Randall Stadium crowd of 78,521 when he raced 83 yards to the Oregon one-yard line on the next play from scrimmage. Brooks Bollinger scored on a one-yard run and the Badgers held on for a 27-23 victory.

"What a day by Michael Bennett," head coach Barry Alvarez said afterward. "It's like a switch came on, and you could just see him get a little more patient, let things happen and then accelerate. He may have just grown up to be a great running back."

Bennett carried 28 times for 290 yards (fourth most in school history at the time) and a pair of touchdowns that day. He averaged a remarkable 10.4 yards per carry. Bennett went on to finish third in the nation in rushing in 2000 with 1,681 yards.

Sorgi to Evans at Michigan State in 2000

Lee Evans caught a school-record 27 touchdown passes in his brilliant career at Wisconsin. He has quarterback Jim Sorgi to thank for 18 of them, and one of the most memorable was the first one at Michigan State.

The Badgers traveled to East Lansing on October 14, 2000, in search of their first conference victory and an end to their three-game losing streak, but things started badly. The Spartans used a 31-yard field goal from David Schaefer and a 43-yard touchdown pass from Ryan Van Dyke to Herb Haygood for a 10-0 lead after the first quarter.

Though he was 0-for-6 passing that afternoon, Badger quarterback Brooks Bollinger scored on a one-yard touchdown run and Vitaly Pisetsky booted a 38-yard field goal in the second quarter to bring the teams to a 10-10 deadlock. The game was still tied when Sorgi, who had taken over in the second half after Bollinger left the game with a concussion, hit Chris Chambers on a nine-yard slant with 46 seconds left to play in regulation. Michael Bennett vaulted through the air for a first down on the next play to set up the game's biggest moment.

The call from the Badger sidelines was a "dog" route, which sent Evans, Chambers and Nick Davis downfield. With Chambers commanding the Spartans' attention, Sorgi looked off the safety in the middle of the field and lofted a strike to Evans, who pulled the ball in and glided into the end zone with 29 seconds left.

"The crazy thing was that ball had never come to me on that play, not in practice, never," Evans said. "For me, as a sophomore, it was incredible."

As Sorgi was performing his heroics, fans at Fraser (Michigan) High School's homecoming game that afternoon were cheering him

Lee Evans caught a school-record 27 touchdown passes during his career.
Photo by David Stluka

on. The public address announcer had been keeping the crowd at Sorgi's prep alma mater updated on the happenings at Spartan Stadium.

"I remember doing an interview on the field after the game," Sorgi said. "Then I did the postgame press conference. I remember my grandma calling me on the bus and telling me she had called the press box because they were pronouncing my name wrong. The whole day was just a great memory for me."

2001: A Very Strange Season

A weather delay, a postponement due to terrorism, an accident outside Camp Randall Stadium on gameday, and an assortment of memorable victories and defeats made the 2001 Badger football season one of the most unusual in recent memory.

The campaign started on August 25 when the Badgers hosted Virginia in the Eddie Robinson Classic in Madison. Strong thunderstorms rolled through the area, however, and the start of the game was delayed 37 minutes. Fans were provided shelter in areas around the stadium, and the Badgers eventually won the contest 26-17.

Back-to-back losses at seventh-ranked Oregon and at home against surprising 19th-ranked Fresno State left the Badgers with a 1-2 mark. Then came September 11.

Wisconsin was scheduled to host Western Kentucky on Saturday, September 15, but that game was postponed until September 29 after the terrorist attacks in New York and Washington, D.C. The Badgers' first post-September 11 game was at Penn State on September 22 and they soundly defeated the Nittany Lions, 18-6. UW seemed to be back on track after defeating Western Kentucky at home and preparing to host Indiana.

The Hoosiers, who entered the October 6 game with an 0-3 mark, shocked everyone in Camp Randall Stadium by moving out to a 32-0 lead after the first quarter. Led by Levron Williams's 280 rushing yards and six touchdowns, IU routed the Badgers, 63-32. Wisconsin then turned around the following week and won a 20-17 decision at Ohio State, giving the Badgers victories in Happy Valley and Columbus in less than a month's time.

Wisconsin won just one more game that season, a 34-28 verdict at home over Iowa on November 3. That morning 11 fans were hit by a taxi cab at the corner of Breese Terrace and Old University Avenue as they headed to the game. They were transported to area hospitals.

A Stormy Start

The 2001 season turned out to be full of many odd twists and turns for the Badger football program so, in hindsight, it should not be shocking to recall the bizarre way it began.

Wisconsin was scheduled to host Virginia at 1:00 p.m. in the Eddie Robinson Classic, an early-season contest (August 25) played to honor the game's legendary namesake, who coached 55 years at Grambling.

Mother Nature, however, had other ideas. Three strong storm cells were scheduled to roll through Madison late that morning. UW game management officials, headed by first-year assistant athletic director Doug Beard, decided to open the stadium gates to fans at the standard time (90 minutes before kickoff). The first storm cell hit at about 11:30 a.m., so fans were kept sheltered in the UW Field House, McClain Center, Camp Randall Memorial Sports Center (The Shell) and throughout the stadium concourses.

Meanwhile, the teams were stranded in the locker rooms, all dressed up with no place to go. "Everybody was all revved up and ready to go," said defensive tackle Wendell Bryant. "We just had to wait. I didn't think we were ever going to play that game. It was really annoying."

Game officials, however, had no choice.

"The cells kept coming through," Beard said. "Just after 1:00 p.m., we met with both coaches and we were looking at the radar screen and there were a couple more cells headed our way. We had decided that if those hit, we were going to postpone the game. They ended up going just south, and by the second half the sun was out."

The delay lasted 37 minutes. The teams came back to the field, warmed up for about 15 minutes and began playing with less than 10,000 fans in their seats. The Badgers survived Virginia's game-opening 61-yard kickoff return, took a 10-3 halftime lead, and went on to a 26-17 victory.

September 11 Cancels Games

A generation of Americans will always remember where they were and what they were doing on November 22, 1963, the day President John F. Kennedy was assassinated in Dallas. The tragedy was a watershed event in 20th century U.S. history.

By the middle of the morning of Tuesday, September 11, 2001, another generation of Americans had a date that they, too, would forever recall in chilling detail. It was the day terrorists hijacked four American commercial jets, crashing two of them into the World Trade Center in New York and another into the Pentagon in Washington, D.C. The fourth plane crashed in a field in Pennsylvania after its passengers had apparently fought back against the terrorists for control of the aircraft.

Most college students on campuses across the country were either still sleeping or were attending early classes. Members of the Badger football team were no different.

"I remember I was heading to a class and saw a friend of mine who asked me if I had heard what happened," recalled defensive lineman Wendell Bryant, whose birthday is on September 12. "I ended up in Grainger Hall watching it all on television. We saw that other plane hit [in New York] and then they flashed on the screen that another plane had crashed into the Pentagon. It was just an emotional, trying day."

No Division IA college football games were played on Saturday, September 15. The Badgers were scheduled to host Western Kentucky that day, but the game was moved to September 29, which originally was Wisconsin's open date on the schedule. Instead the Badgers practiced on the north practice field outside Camp Randall

Stadium under a sunny sky much like the one in New York four days earlier.

September 11 Hits Close to Home

Wisconsin had opened the 2001 season with a victory over Virginia, but lost its next two games to teams—Oregon and Fresno State—that were led by future first-round draft choices Joey Harrington and David Carr.

The Badger coaching staff was conducting its regular Tuesday morning meetings in preparation for the upcoming game with Western Kentucky when Director of Football Operations John Chadima interrupted with the startling news that a plane had crashed into the World Trade Center in New York.

"We all got up to start watching the news," offensive coordinator Brian White said. "Then the second plane hit as we were watching it."

White's first thought was that his brother, Kevin, was employed by Lehman Brothers, Inc., as a managing director in a building (the World Financial Center) across the street from, but connected to, the World Trade Center. White was not even entertaining the thought that the buildings might come down.

"I'm trying to reach my brother, but his cell phone isn't working," White said. "Then the buildings go down and now I'm calling my mom, my dad, everyone. No one had heard from my brother."

It was about 1:00 p.m. that day that the White family finally received an e-mail stating simply: "I'm OK. I'll talk to you later."

Trying to Return to Normal

The days following the September 11, 2001, terrorist attacks were marked by a wide range of emotions: uncertainty, anger, sadness, fear. President George W. Bush, however, had been telling Americans to get back to the business of living their lives. Part of that return to "normalcy" was a resumption of sporting activities.

Wisconsin's first football game after September 11 was its Big Ten opener at Penn State on September 22. As significant as it was to start playing games again, it also was important to pause to remember what had shaken the world 11 days earlier, and Penn State's athletic department did that with class.

Both teams were on the field at Beaver Stadium for the playing and singing of both the national anthem and "God Bless America." A large flag covered much of the playing field and the pregame activity included a video tribute. Both teams met at midfield to shake hands prior to kickoff.

Wisconsin won the low-scoring game, 18-6, as defensive tackle Wendell Bryant tied a then school record with six tackles for loss, including five quarterback sacks. Freshman running back Anthony Davis registered the first 200-yard rushing game of his career with a 37-carry, 200-yard effort and quarterback Brooks Bollinger contributed 112 yards on the ground.

"I really felt our players gave attention to where it was needed," head coach Barry Alvarez said after the game. "When it was time to concentrate on football, they gave us tremendous focus. When it was time to show sympathy and have prayers for the victims and survivors, they were into that."

Phone Call from a Friend

Just a few months had gone by since Lee Evans's world had changed the instant he tore his anterior cruciate ligament in his left knee in the Badgers' 2002 spring game at Camp Randall Stadium. The 2001 Biletnikoff Award finalist had set the Big Ten single-season receiving yardage record and opted to return to Wisconsin for his senior year. Now he was spending the summer rehabilitating his knee.

One day his cell phone rang as he relaxed at his Madison apartment. On the other end of the line was none other than perennial Pro Bowl receiver and future NFL Hall of Famer Jerry Rice. The then Oakland Raider star, who had himself come back from knee injuries he sustained in 1997, had been told of Evans's plight and decided to give him a call.

"We didn't talk at length," Evans said. "It was the principle of the call. He didn't have to do it. It was solely at his discretion. It did a lot for me, mentally, at the time. Jerry Rice, my favorite player ever, telling me I was still young and had time to heal up. It was an incredible experience for me."

Rice called Evans again a month later and left another message of encouragement. The two later met in person at the Super Bowl.

The Power Outage

One of the oddest endings to a Badger football game came on August 31, 2002, at UNLV's Sam Boyd Stadium.

Thanks in part to five first-half UNLV turnovers, Wisconsin took a 24-7 halftime lead. The teams played a scoreless third quarter before Badger kicker Scott Campbell added a 42-yard field goal with 7:57 remaining to play in the fourth quarter. Just 16 more seconds ticked off the clock, however, before the game ended prematurely.

The lights in the stadium suddenly went out with 7:41 left to play. Players from both teams stood around on the field in the darkness as game officials, head coaches Barry Alvarez of Wisconsin and John Robinson of UNLV, and officials from the conference offices mulled over what to do.

Auxiliary power kicked in, but it did not provide enough light to continue the game. Approximately 16 minutes elapsed before the contest was called.

"The players had cooled down," Alvarez told the *Wisconsin State Journal* after the game. "We had originally been told by the officials we'd wait five minutes, and if they [lights] did not come back on and the scoreboard did not come on, the game would be over. John [Robinson] and I agreed to that."

Robinson also noted that the safety of the players was an issue. "That late in the game, through standing around for that long of time, your energy dissipates, soreness and stiffness take over."

For some in the crowd of 42,075 (a record for a team sporting event in Nevada), the incident created an uneasy moment of uncertainty, particularly with the first anniversary of the September

11 terrorist attacks less than two weeks away. UNLV police, however, cited a downed transformer as the cause of the outage.

The Great Musket Caper

Wisconsin's second game of the 2002 season, a 27-7 victory at UNLV's Sam Boyd Stadium, ended in darkness with 7:41 left in the fourth quarter after a power outage caused the stadium lights to go out. That should have been the most widely discussed thing the Badgers encountered all season. It wasn't.

The 25th-ranked Badgers, sporting a 2-0 record and looking to continue to gain momentum after a 5-7 campaign the year before, began preparations to host West Virginia the following week.

West Virgina, like most schools, has a mascot. Unlike most schools, however, West Virginia's mascot is a Mountaineer who fires a musket when the Mountaineer football team takes the field, as well as each time the team scores. That fact became a source of controversy that put the Wisconsin-West Virginia game that week on the national college football map.

Early in the week of the game, it came to the attention of Wisconsin officials that West Virginia's mascot would be coming to Camp Randall Stadium with the intention of firing his musket as he always had. UW officials had no problem with the mascot or the gun, as long as the weapon was not fired.

That stance made its way back to West Virginia and spread quickly via internet message boards. Eventually, officials from the University of Wisconsin System cited a policy that would disallow not only the firing of the musket, but the firearm itself, from entering the stadium.

Mountaineer fans were irate. Wisconsin athletic officials, primarily associate athletic director Jamie Pollard, were frustrated and were deluged with phone calls and e-mails, including some from the National Rifle Association (NRA). The national media ate it all up.

"I must have gotten 150 or 200 e-mails, along with phone calls, because it was my name linked to a quote [in the newspaper],"

Pollard said. "I got e-mails from the NRA, and I got nasty phone calls. I sat in my office one night and responded to every single e-mail that was sent to me. The perception was that we weren't going to let him bring the gun. That wasn't the case. We were going to let him bring the gun; we just preferred that he not shoot it."

The fire was put out when UW-Madison Chancellor John Wiley decided to allow the Mountaineer into Camp Randall Stadium with permission to fire the musket. Pollard ended up seeking out the Mountaineer mascot, Trey Hinrichs, the morning of the game, and the pair had their photo taken together.

The ironic twist to the whole saga came later that season when Hinrichs tried to fire the musket during West Virginia's home game with Boston College. The gun did not go off, so Hinrichs turned the gun around and looked down the barrel. That is, of course, when the weapon fired as gunpowder shot into Hinrichs's face.

The Heart of a Winner

Ask someone to describe the stereotypical football player, and you'll hear words like big, strong, tough, and mean. You probably would not hear words such as emotional, caring, or heartfelt. Then again, Brooks Bollinger was not your stereotypical football player.

The quarterback with more wins as a starter than anyone in school history was a poised, competitive leader for the Badgers from 1999-2002. He loved playing football, and he loved Wisconsin, and he told his teammates that the night before his last home game.

"He really spoke from the heart," recalled quarterbacks coach Jeff Horton. "A lot of times men are afraid to show their emotions, because they think that's a sign of weakness, but you could really see what Wisconsin meant to him that night. The message he delivered, the tears that flowed, the belonging that he felt, the relationships he developed, what the University had done for him, how he felt being a member of the football team, all those things came into play."

Bollinger and the Badgers went out the next day and locked up a bid to the 2002 Alamo Bowl with a 49-31 victory over rival Minnesota at Camp Randall Stadium.

Bollinger Refuses to Lose

Wisconsin won its first five games of the 2002 season and looked poised to return to the bowl scene after finishing out of the postseason picture with a 5-7 record the year before. The Badgers, however, dropped six of their next seven games and entered the regular-season finale needing a victory just to qualify for a bowl game.

The Badgers' last game of the 2002 regular season was played in a chilly Camp Randall Stadium against archrival Minnesota. In addition to the game's bowl implications, the Badgers would be trying to win back the fabled Paul Bunyan Axe, the trophy that annually goes to the winner of the game between the two schools.

The Badgers trailed on three separate occasions that day, including a 31-28 deficit that they faced early in the fourth quarter. Quarterback Brooks Bollinger and tailback Anthony Davis, however, would not let Wisconsin lose. In the last 11 minutes of the game, Bollinger directed touchdown drives of 75, 75, and 80 yards to give the Badgers a 49-31 victory. Davis rushed 45 times for 301 yards and five touchdowns, while Bollinger contributed 112 yards rushing and another 134 yards passing.

"Brooks said the night before there was no way we were going to lose that football game, that he was going to put it on his shoulders and get it done," recalled Jeff Horton, Bollinger's position coach. "And he did, obviously with a lot of help, but he played one of his best games ever."

The victory was Bollinger's 29th as the starting quarterback at Wisconsin and made him the winningest signalcaller in school history.

Davis Duplicates Marek

The similarities are uncanny. Badger running backs Billy Marek and Anthony Davis had nearly identical performances exactly 28 years apart against the same opponent.

Anthony Davis finished his career as the school's No. 2 all-time rusher.
Photo by David Stluka

Marek set the school record for rushing yards and touchdowns in a game when he carried 43 times for 304 yards and five touchdowns in a 49-14 victory over Minnesota in the regular-season finale at Camp Randall Stadium on November 23, 1974.

Davis practically copied Marek's effort with a 45-carry, 301-yard, five-touchdown showing in a 49-31 win against the Golden Gophers in the last regular-season game in Madison on November 23, 2002.

Neither player was ever given to self-promotion. Marek credited his offensive line for opening large holes through which he ran all day against the Golden Gophers. And Davis had to be reached for postgame comment via cell phone at a restaurant following his performance against Minnesota. He had left the stadium under the assumption that he wouldn't be asked to meet with the media.

The History Lesson

Jeff Horton, the Wisconsin quarterbacks coach since 1999, was not born in Texas, but he grew up there and considers himself a Texan, because his parents were both born there. So he took notice when he learned some of the Badger players were not familiar with the story of the Alamo.

"What disturbed me was when we first landed in San Antonio for the Alamo Bowl [in 2002], the media were asking our players what the Alamo meant to them, and one of the players didn't know what the Alamo was," Horton recalled. "I knew, as a Texan, that they would take that as an insult down there. It would be like telling someone from Wisconsin that they didn't know what cheddar cheese was."

Horton told head coach Barry Alvarez that, if there was time, he would like the opportunity to tell the Badgers the story of one of the legendary events in Texas history. Alvarez obliged and called Horton up in front of the team after practice a couple days before the game.

"I tried to tie the game into the story because the Mexican army was a heavy favorite to defeat the Texans, just like the University of Colorado was favored to beat us," Horton said. "Nobody gave the Texas volunteers a chance, just like they weren't giving us a chance."

The most entertaining moment of the history lesson came when Horton recounted a key moment during the siege. He told the players that Colonel William B. Travis is said to have drawn a line in the dirt and urged those who wanted to stay and fight to step over.

"All but one guy stepped over the line, and the one who didn't got sent to Colorado," Horton said as the players chuckled at his embellishment.

The Badgers upset the 14th-ranked Buffaloes, 31-28, when Mike Allen kicked a 37-yard field goal in overtime.

Remember The Alamo

The 2002 regular season had started and ended with a victory, but in between were six wins and five losses, so the Badgers were happy to be playing in a quality bowl game like the Alamo Bowl in San Antonio. They would, however, have their work cut out for them with 14th-ranked Colorado (9-4 overall) as their opponent.

Quarterback Brooks Bollinger had led the Badgers to 29 victories during his career as a starter, but his final game in a Wisconsin uniform got off to a rough start. Bollinger drove the Badgers to the Colorado 17-yard line on the game's opening series, only to have Don Strickland intercept a pass and take it 91 yards for a
touchdown.

The Badgers responded, however, and took a 21-14 lead at the half. Colorado then countered with a pair of third-quarter touchdowns, and the Buffaloes held a 28-21 edge as Wisconsin took over on its own 20-yard line with 2:25 left to play in the fourth quarter. Bollinger went to work.

He completed a 32-yard pass to freshman Brandon Williams on the first play of the drive and then, faced with a fourth-and-18 situation from the Wisconsin 44-yard line, connected with Williams again for 27 yards to the Colorado 29-yard line. Three straight incomplete passes followed before Bollinger converted a fourth-and-10 by hitting sophomore Darrin Charles on a 28-yard pass. Bollinger dove in from the one-yard line on the next play to send the game into overtime with just 51 seconds left.

The Badgers won the overtime coin toss and elected to play defense. They forced the Buffaloes into a 45-yard field-goal attempt that kicker Pat Brougham pushed wide right. The Badgers then rushed for five yards, and sophomore walk-on kicker Mike Allen booted the game-winning, 37-yard field goal.

"I got it in my head that there was no way we were going to lose that game," Bollinger recalled years later. "I tried to express that to the guys on the team. I didn't care what happened early in the game. I never wavered from the feeling we would win."

The victory was Bollinger's school-record 30th as the Badgers' starting quarterback. His direction of Wisconsin's fourth-quarter comeback further cemented his place as one of the great leaders and clutch performers in school history.

"Brooks was a unique player," said head coach Barry Alvarez. "He was a gym rat. He was a fierce competitor, he loved to practice, and he loved to play. Our last two games of his career, he refused to lose."

The Comeback

Few players in Badger football history experienced the physical and emotional peaks and valleys that wide receiver Lee Evans did. And few, if any, handled those extremes with more grace and maturity than Wisconsin's career receiving leader.

Evans came to Wisconsin as a freshman in 1999, joining former Bedford (Ohio) High School teammate and fellow Badger receiving great Chris Chambers in Madison. Evans played as a true freshman for the Badgers' 1999 Big Ten and 2000 Rose Bowl championship team before becoming the team's second-leading receiver as a sophomore. It was a solid start to his career, but nothing like what was to come in 2001.

Evans's junior year with the Badgers was simply remarkable. On his way to first-team All-America honors, Evans set the Big Ten record for receiving yards in a season with 1,545. He set school records for receptions in a season (75), touchdown receptions in a season (tied with nine) and 100-yard receiving games in a season (eight). One of three finalists for the Fred Biletnikoff Award as the nation's best receiver, Evans had become Wisconsin's career receiving yardage leader after just three seasons.

Then in January of 2002, with speculation swirling about whether he would declare for the National Football League draft, Evans announced that he would return to Wisconsin for his senior year. "It mostly has to do with me improving as a person," Evans said of his decision. "And being able to mature and go to the next level when I get the chance and be able to handle it the right way."

Evans would, indeed, come to mature and improve as a person, but not in the manner he expected. The unthinkable happened when he went up to catch a pass during the Badgers' spring game at Camp Randall Stadium on the same day as the NFL draft. He came down with the ball but tore the anterior cruciate ligament in his left knee.

"There were a million things running through my mind at one time," Evans recalled of the moment the injury occurred. "You're in disbelief, you're trying to be optimistic. It was like, that quick, everything that was, was not anymore. That's how fast things can turn."

Evans had surgery on May 22, 2002, with an eye toward playing that fall. He rehabilitated the knee all summer but never was able to get back on the field. Doctors performed a second surgery on November 22. Evans ended up redshirting during the 2002 season and announced at the 2002 Alamo Bowl that he would return to Wisconsin for his final season.

Among those who helped Evans on his road to recovery was John Dettmann, the Badgers' strength and conditioning coach. "My message, initially, was 'No matter what it takes, whatever time we have to spend, whatever we've got to do, we'll get you back,'" Dettmann said. "The reality of it is that it's a day-to-day process. You can't look too far ahead, you can only look ahead to the next day.

You try to make small increases on a daily basis and, mentally, that kills you. Being the mature kid that he was and the mentally strong kid that he was is why he was able to handle it better than others might."

"I can't put into words all that he did for me," Evans said of Dettmann. "He was someone I saw every day. We stayed in constant contact. He was in my corner tremendously. Without him, I don't know if I would have made it all the way back as strong as I did."

And make it back strong is exactly what he did. Evans made 64 catches for 1,213 yards and a school-record 13 touchdowns as a senior. Among his performances that year were: a 99-yard touchdown catch against Akron; a game-winning, 79-yard touchdown catch against third-ranked Ohio State; and a record-breaking, 10-catch, 258-yard, five-touchdown performance against Michigan State. He left Wisconsin ranked second on the Big Ten's career receiving yardage (3,468) list.

"Lee was just a special person to be around," head coach Barry Alvarez said. "He went through so much adversity. We all learned from him. He never got down, and if there was anybody that had a right to be bitter or negative, it was Lee. But you never saw that with him. He just made things work. He stayed positive and he was an inspiration to all of us."

Evans's journey at Wisconsin was completed when the Buffalo Bills selected him in the first round (13th overall) of the 2004 NFL Draft. He led all NFL rookies with nine touchdown catches in 2004.

56 Jerk

Camp Randall Stadium hosted nearly 500 Wisconsin football games from 1917-2004. Few, if any, were more dramatic than the 2003 contest against Ohio State, which may have been the most anticipated game in Madison since Ron Dayne broke the NCAA career rushing record against Iowa in November of 1999.

The third-ranked Buckeyes were the defending national champions and, led by the country's top-ranked run defense, were riding a 19-game winning streak. Wisconsin, ranked No. 23

nationally, was 5-1 overall (2-0 in Big Ten play), but was without injured tailback Anthony Davis. ESPN's *Prime Time* crew was in town to telecast the game slated for an 8:00 p.m. start.

"It was the most incredible atmosphere I've ever played in or seen," recalled wide receiver Lee Evans. "Down-in and down-out, that atmosphere was the best. So much was riding on that game and so much went into it."

Rain fell as the two teams slugged it out through a scoreless first quarter. Then, on the first play of the second quarter, Badger redshirt freshman tailback Booker Stanley punctuated a 13-play, 63-yard scoring drive with a two-yard touchdown run. Mike Allen's point-after attempt was good, and Wisconsin led 7-0.

Ohio State's Mike Nugent kicked a 24-yard field goal in the second quarter, and the Badgers took a 7-3 lead at the half. The Buckeyes gained just 62 yards in the first two quarters.

The two teams traded turnovers early in the third quarter, but only the Badgers came away with points. Badger long snapper Matt Katula recovered Chris Gamble's fumbled punt return at Ohio State's 38-yard line with 8:19 left in the quarter. Wisconsin ended up with a 38-yard Allen field goal, but the Badgers lost starting quarterback Jim Sorgi in the process.

One play before Allen's field goal, Sorgi had gained eight yards on third down and 15 from the Ohio State 28-yard line. Buckeye linebacker Robert Reynolds then pressed his hand down on Sorgi's throat, effectively choking the Badger quarterback. Sorgi left the field under his own power, but did not return to the game.

The Badgers maintained their 10-3 lead until Ohio State quarterback Craig Krenzel orchestrated a seven-play, 75-yard scoring drive that ended with a six-yard touchdown pass to Michael Jenkins with 6:09 left in the fourth quarter. The Buckeyes had won 10 games by seven points or less during their winning streak and had put themselves in position to get No. 11.

But it wasn't to be. Evans and Badger backup quarterback Matt Schabert, replacing the injured Sorgi, saw to that. Wisconsin took over at its own 20-yard line with 6:09 left to play in the fourth quarter. Stanley carried for one yard on first down before Schabert and Evans sent a jolt through Camp Randall Stadium.

It was second down and nine. "I didn't have a catch, didn't have a ball thrown to me [yet that night] and I knew people were waiting on me to do something," Evans remembered. "It [the play call] was a 56 Jerk, out and up. I remember running the route, seeing him [Ohio State's Gamble] bite and turning it upfield, and all I was thinking was, 'The ball better come up.'" It did. Schabert fired a perfect strike to Evans, who streaked down the field for a 79-yard touchdown and one of the most memorable plays in Badger history.

Wisconsin forced the Buckeyes to punt on their ensuing possession and the Badgers ran out the clock. Stanley carried 31 times for 125 yards and one touchdown as the Badgers churned out 141 rushing yards against the vaunted Buckeye defense. On the flip side, Wisconsin shut down the Buckeye ground game, limiting Ohio State to just 69 yards rushing and 271 yards in total offense.

Sorgi to Evans: Five Times

For quarterback Jim Sorgi and wide receiver Lee Evans, it was like driving to work and making every traffic light. It was a birdie on every hole, a base hit every time at bat.

There may never have been a greater two-player performance in Wisconsin history than the one Sorgi and Evans put on against Michigan State on a gray November afternoon at Camp Randall Stadium in 2003.

The Badgers had lost three straight games by a total of 15 points and needed a victory as they battled to position themselves for a bowl appearance.

Sorgi was coming off the best performance of his career, having completed 23-of-34 passes for 305 yards and four touchdowns in a 37-34 loss at Minnesota the week before. Evans was feeling increasingly confident as the season progressed, his rehabilitated knee getting stronger and stronger. However, neither player could have imagined they would play about as perfect a game as is possible against the Spartans that day.

Wisconsin cruised to a 28-7 halftime lead after Sorgi delivered touchdown passes of nine, 75, and 18 yards to Evans. The two seniors hooked up for aerial scores of 70 and 18 yards in the third quarter to give the Badgers a 42-14 lead entering the final stanza.

"I remember being out of the game by the start of the fourth quarter and thinking that the game was taking forever," said Sorgi, who completed 16-of-24 passes for 380 yards and five touchdowns, in addition to setting the school single-game record for pass efficiency (268.4). "It was probably the cleanest and most productive football game I've ever played."

Evans ended up with 10 receptions for school records of 258 yards and five touchdowns.

"It was one of those days where nothing went wrong," Evans said. "I caught every ball that was thrown to me. I remember one that was incomplete because I was out of bounds, but I caught the ball. He [Sorgi] was in a zone, I was in a zone, and we were clicking. It was special. That was probably the most fun I've ever had playing football."

So remarkable was the Sorgi-Evans performance that it "overshadowed" a 207-yard, three-touchdown rushing effort that afternoon by Badger sophomore Dwayne Smith.

Incidentally, Evans's career statistics against Michigan State were mind-boggling: 20 receptions, 531 yards and nine touchdowns (exactly one-third of his career total of 27).

The Rusty Tool Box

"Trophy Games" are plentiful in college football. There is Paul Bunyan's Axe (Wisconsin-Minnesota), the Little Brown Jug (Minnesota-Michigan), the Old Oaken Bucket (Purdue-Indiana), the Megaphone Trophy (Michigan State-Notre Dame) and many more. There is also the Rusty Tool Box.

John Chadima, now an associate athletic director at Wisconsin, was a football student manager as an undergraduate at Iowa in the mid-1980s. Chadima went to Wisconsin as coach Barry Alvarez's administrative assistant in 1990 and was assigned the task of overseeing the Badger football student managers.

Chadima, now with ties to both Iowa and Wisconsin, conferred with his old boss at Iowa, administrative associate Bill Dervrich, and the two created the Rusty Tool Box to be awarded to the winner of the two schools' annual student manager flag football game that is held the night before the two football teams meet. The "trophy" is an old tool box, half red and white and half black and gold with game scores listed. The winning team's logo is placed on the tool box, which is kept with the program that has won the game until they meet again.

Several of the games have been extremely competitive and hotly contested. In fact, two of the Badger managers collided with each other while diving for an Iowa flag during the 2004 game in Iowa City. Both of them spent the night in the hospital.

Persistence Pays Off

Ask Badger veteran offensive line coach Jim Hueber about the most memorable or interesting players he has coached at Wisconsin, and several of the school's most successful on-field performers are named: Joe Panos, Mike Samuel, Brent Moss, Chris McIntosh.

Hueber has another one, too. It's offensive lineman Mike Lorenz.

"I don't know how gifted an athlete or player he was," Hueber said of Lorenz. "But what he accomplished here, earning his degree with two classes in the first semester of his fifth year, finding a way to get on the field and overcoming the obstacle he had with his [reading disorder]. He was truly a testament to the fact that hard work can get you where you want to go. The big thing about Mike was he found a way to get what he wanted."

Lorenz, a product of Manitowoc, Wisconsin, was diagnosed with dyslexia when he was in grade school. That made comprehending what he was reading or writing or hearing more difficult than it was for others.

But Lorenz persevered. By his senior year in high school, he had finally earned a 3.0 grade-point average (and the 40-ounce steak his brother, Tom, had promised to buy him for doing so). He also had earned a scholarship to play football for the Badgers.

Lorenz was not a star player at Wisconsin, but he saw action in 35 games during his career, including starting his entire junior year at right tackle and splitting time at that position with Morgan Davis his senior year. He was a solid, three-time letterwinner.

Ironically, it was in the classroom where Lorenz did star. He was a three-time Academic All-Big Ten selection and participated in commencement ceremonies in December of 2004.

No. 100

Head coach Barry Alvarez's 100th win at Wisconsin originally looked like it would come sometime in late October or November during the 2003 season. He had won No. 98 when the Badgers upset third-ranked Ohio State, 17-10, on October 11. Five regular-season games, plus a bowl game, remained.

Wisconsin, however, won just once more that season. That left Alvarez with 99 victories heading into the 2004 campaign.

The Badgers opened the 2004 season at home against Central Florida, and they left no doubt that they would get their coach his 100th victory. Wisconsin cruised to a 34-6 win and Alvarez left the field to chants of "Barry, Barry, Barry."

"The only thing I can think of is all the people that were involved in it, how many people since 1990, where the program was, and how far it has come and what we've accomplished," Alvarez said after the game.

Alvarez became just the 10th coach in Big Ten history to reach 100 wins at one conference institution. In doing so he joined the likes of Amos Alonzo Stagg, Woody Hayes, Bo Schembechler, Hayden Fry, and Duffy Daugherty, among others.

A Desert Storm

All during the week leading up to Wisconsin's non-conference game at Arizona in September of 2004, the talk had centered on whether or not the Badgers would be able to play under the heat of the desert sun, particularly given the fact that kickoff had been moved to 1:00 p.m. for television.

The last thing anyone had planned on was a thunderstorm, accompanied by lightning, that would cause an 88-minute delay with 6:31 left to play in the second quarter. But that is exactly what happened.

The Badgers and Wildcats had battled to a scoreless tie when the storm forced the teams off the field and fans out of Arizona Stadium. As rainwater caused flooding in the Wisconsin locker room, game officials discussed their options. A break in the severity of the weather allowed the game to resume, but Wisconsin head coach Barry Alvarez and Arizona head coach Mike Stoops agreed via cell phone from their respective locker rooms to skip halftime to make sure they were able to get the game in.

The Wildcats scored on a 44-yard touchdown pass with 32 seconds left in the second quarter for a 7-0 lead. The Badgers finally got on the board when running back Booker Stanley, who rushed for a career-high 135 yards that day, carried for a seven-yard touchdown with 14:21 left in the fourth quarter. But kicker Mike Allen's extra-point attempt was wide right, leaving the Badgers with a 7-6 deficit.

A 16-play, 72-yard drive that consumed 7:26 and included two third-down conversions and one fourth-down attempt culminated in a 23-yard Allen field goal with just 3:47 left to play that gave Wisconsin a 9-7 lead. Arizona, however, was not quite finished.

The Wildcats drove to the Wisconsin 25-yard line on their ensuing possession before losing five yards. That left Wildcat sophomore kicker Nick Folk, who had already missed a 43-yard attempt that would have given Arizona a 10-9 lead, facing a 47-yard try.

Folk's potential game-winning kick missed to the left. The Badgers had survived a stubborn opponent as well as a rare desert storm.

A Hoagie and an I.V.

Anyone looking to assess the strengths of the 2004 Wisconsin football team prior to the start of fall camp would have given high marks to the Badger running backs.

A healthy senior Anthony Davis was expected to be on the Heisman Trophy radar screen. Junior Dwayne Smith was the Badgers' leading rusher in 2003 (he had substituted for Davis, who had battled ankle injuries all year). Sophomore Booker Stanley had also contributed in 2003, rushing for more than 100 yards three times and earning the team's rookie of the year award.

It was unimaginable that Wisconsin would need a career-high, 123-yard rushing performance from junior fullback Matt Bernstein to help it to a 16-7 victory over Penn State under the lights in the Big Ten opener at Camp Randall Stadium on September 25. That is, however, just what happened.

Smith's career was unexpectedly brought to an end before the season even started due to a heart ailment that doctors discovered during a physical exam. Davis sustained an eye injury in the second quarter of the season opener against Central Florida and missed the next three games, including Penn State. Stanley started the Penn State game, but left with turf toe. Freshman Jamil Walker spelled Stanley but departed with a shoulder injury.

Enter Bernstein, a six-foot-three, 270-pounder, who admittedly had never played tailback. Combine that with the fact that his previous season high for rushing yards was 120 during his sophomore year in 2003, and the story would have been plenty good. But there was more.

Bernstein had fasted for 24 hours starting on Friday at 5:00 p.m. in observance of Yom Kippur, the Jewish Day of Atonement (he actually began his fast two hours early so he could play in the game, which kicked off at 4:45 p.m. on Saturday). He did not participate in warmups with the Badgers. Instead of the traditional Jewish "Break the Fast" fare of eggs, bagels or smoked salmon, Bernstein had a pregame I.V. and ate oranges and slices of turkey. Wisconsin moved out to a 13-0 halftime lead, but had gained just 13 yards on 18 carries in the first half.

Offensive coordinator and running backs coach Brian White called on Bernstein to start the second half at tailback, and the junior from Scarsdale, New York, responded by gaining 62 of Wisconsin's 73 yards on an opening drive that consumed the first 7:59 of the third quarter and resulted in a 26-yard field goal by Mike Allen and gave the Badgers a 16-0 lead.

The Wisconsin defense smothered the Nittany Lions the rest of the way, as Bernstein became the third different Badger in four games to rush for 100 yards. Asked after the game how Bernstein had satisfied his hunger after the fast, head coach Barry Alvarez joked, "We gave him a hoagie and an I.V."

The Benefit of Cold Weather

One of defensive line coach John Palermo's top recruits and, later one of his top players, was tackle Anttaj Hawthorne. The 300-pound Hawthorne was a highly touted high school player and could have played his college ball just about anywhere he wanted. One of the reasons he liked Wisconsin was the weather. The weather?

"Anttaj is the only guy that I've ever been around or recruited who wanted to play in cold weather," Palermo said. "He could have gone to Miami, Florida State, anywhere in the South. But he didn't want to play in the heat. He said he wanted to play someplace where the weather was colder, and I told him [Wisconsin] was the perfect place for him."

Hawthorne played in 50 of a possible 51 games from 2001-2004, including 42 starts. He was a two-time first-team All-Big Ten selection.

The Fumble Return

Ask 10 Badger fans to create a list of the most memorable plays in Wisconsin football history and you're likely to get 10 different lists. One play, however, that you might find on all 10 is Scott Starks's fumble return at Purdue in 2004.

The Badgers reeled off six straight wins to start the 2004 season and, after a 24-13 victory at 15th-ranked Ohio State on October 9, prepared to travel to fifth-ranked Purdue for what would be the game of the day in college football. Purdue, its high-powered offensive attack led by quarterback and Heisman Trophy candidate Kyle Orton, also had started 6-0.

The atmosphere in West Lafayette was electric. It was Homecoming. ESPN's popular *College Gameday* show, with hosts Chris Fowler, Kirk Herbstreit, and Lee Corso, was broadcasting live from the Purdue campus. It was the nation's top-ranked scoring defense against the highest-scoring team in the country. Wisconsin head coach Barry Alvarez referred to the matchup as "the Jetsons against the Flintstones."

Scott Starks returned a fumble 40 yards for the game-winning touchdown at Purdue in 2004. *Photo by David Stluka*

The 10th-ranked Badgers, keyed by their stifling defense, took a 7-0 lead at the half. Wisconsin's dominating defensive end, Erasmus James, had terrorized the Boilermakers, sacking Orton, forcing a fumble and causing an interception after hitting the Purdue quarterback's arm. The Boilermakers gained just 122 yards in the first half, but things changed when Badger defensive end Jonathan Welsh left the game with a second-quarter ankle injury and James did the same in the third quarter.

Orton proceeded to guide Purdue to two touchdowns and a field goal to give the Boilermakers a 17-7 lead that they held when Wisconsin took over with eight minutes left to play. The Badger comeback started when quarterback John Stocco took his team on a 73-yard scoring drive that consumed 2:31. It was 17-14, and all Purdue had to do was make a few first downs and the game would be over.

The Boilermakers received the ensuing kickoff, eventually moving to their own 37-yard line, where they faced third down and three. Orton ran a bootleg to his right and appeared to have picked up the first down, but he was upended by Starks and fellow Badger defensive back Robert Brooks. Brooks knocked the ball loose, and Starks scooped it up and raced 40 yards for a touchdown with 2:36 remaining to play. Purdue then added to the suspense when it blocked Mike Allen's extra-point attempt, leaving the Badgers with a 20-17 lead.

Orton took the Boilermakers back down the field in a desperate attempt to at least send the game into overtime, but Ben Jones's 42-yard field goal attempt with 24 seconds left went wide right. The Badgers had locked up one of the most improbable fourth-quarter comeback victories in school history.

"I've been in this racket a long time," Alvarez said after the game. "I don't know if I've ever been in a game like that."

Starks's play, incidentally, was voted by college football fans as the "Pontiac Game Changing Play of the Year," securing a $100,000 award to the University of Wisconsin's general scholarship fund. The UW Department of Athletics used the money to help endow an athletic scholarship in the names of Starks and Brooks.

Matt Lepay's Most Memorable Games

Matt Lepay, the state of Wisconsin's sportscaster of the year in 1997, 2000, 2003 and 2004, has been the radio play-by-play voice for Badger football since 1994 and prior to that hosted pregame, halftime and postgame shows. He has called many of the great games of the Barry Alvarez era. Here are some of Lepay's favorites, along with his comments:

1999 Iowa game: "I've never witnessed such hype before a Wisconsin football game. Even with three Rose Bowl wins in the Alvarez era, the "Dayne Game" stands out because it was a home game. Normally, when I arrive at the stadium three hours before a game, it's easy to get into the parking lot. Not that day. People were everywhere, and traffic was a challenge. The fact Wisconsin won the [Big Ten] title outright, Dayne broke the [NCAA rushing] record and the Badgers won, 41-3, made it perhaps the closest thing to a perfect day a Badger fan has ever enjoyed."

1994 Rose Bowl against UCLA: "If you've ever watched a Rose Bowl game on television, you've noticed that classic scene in the fourth quarter. A perfect Southern California day gives way to a little haze fighting through the stadium lights. It's almost surreal. The fact that the Badgers and more than 70,000 UW fans were actually there in person was also surreal. I can't tell you how many fans told me they had chills when, earlier in the day, they attended the Rose Parade and cheered the UW Band as it made its way down Colorado Boulevard. It was as though the entire state of Wisconsin was living a dream. When the Badgers stopped UCLA quarterback Wayne Cook on the game's final play, it was so loud I swore the field was shaking. I'm not kidding. For a couple seconds, I thought it was an earthquake."

1999 Rose Bowl against UCLA: "Many coaches need an enemy. Barry Alvarez is no exception, and he didn't have to look far to find one. When television analyst Craig James called Wisconsin the worst team to ever play in the Rose Bowl, you might say the locals were a bit fired up. The game was terrific. Ron Dayne ran wild, and Jamar Fletcher's interception return for a touchdown proved to be the difference. What some people might forget is that

UCLA very nearly played for the national title, but the Bruins dropped their final regular-season game to Miami. Otherwise, the Badgers would have played Arizona."

The Story of Jimmy

The Barry Alvarez Era at Wisconsin has produced a plethora of terrific games, players, and stories. One of its greatest players and stories is safety Jim Leonhard.

A native of Tony, Wisconsin, a small town (population 105) in the northwest part of the state, Leonhard was a multisport star at Flambeau High School. He had no Division I football scholarship offers, but decided to walk-on with the Badgers in the fall of 2001. It would be an understatement to say that decision benefited both Leonhard and the Badgers.

Jim Leonhard became one of the best stories in college football. *Photo by David Stluka*

"His awareness made him special," Alvarez said. "He's one of those guys. He's the shortstop, he's the point guard, has a feel for the game, always around the ball. He was one of the great stories in college football."

Though just five-foot-eight, 180 pounds, Leonhard played his way onto the Badgers' special teams units as a true freshman in 2001, saw action in all 12 games and made 12 tackles. The best, however, was yet to come.

Leonhard became a starter at strong safety as a sophomore and ended up starting all 39 games during his final three seasons (the last two years at free safety). A three-time, first-team All-Big Ten selection, he led the nation in interceptions with a Big Ten record-tying 11 in 2002 and went on to tie Jamar Fletcher's school record for career interceptions with 21.

Leonhard, who twice won the football team's basketball slam dunk competition, also excelled as a punt returner. He twice broke the school season record for punt return yardage and left the UW as the Big Ten record-holder for career punt return yards with 1,347.

A two-time team captain, Leonhard also was a standout off the field. He earned Academic All-Big Ten honors three times, and by his senior year he was selected to CoSIDA's *ESPN The Magazine* Academic All-America first team. He was a finalist for the inaugural Ronnie Lott Trophy in 2004 and won a prestigious $18,000 postgraduate scholarship from the National Football Foundation.

Leonhard was named to at least one first-team All-America squad each of his final three seasons. In a program that has produced dozens of successful walk-on stories, Leonhard's is arguably the most memorable, considering his accomplishments on and off the field.

The Seminary

Wisconsin's football team had one of the most unique preseason training camp arrangements in college football from the early 1970s through 2004. The Badgers prepared for each new season during that period at Holy Name Seminary (later the Bishop O'Connor Catholic Center) in Middleton, Wisconsin.

The facility, located about 15 minutes to the southwest of the UW-Madison campus, was well-equipped to house the Badgers for two weeks or so in August each year.

"The Seminary got going with the Badgers when Father Art Koth was the athletic director at the Seminary," Father Mike Burke said. "He got some of the moms [of the seminarians] to cook for the football team. It was a fundraiser for the athletic department of the seminary."

Indeed, the arrangement became a significant source of revenue for the seminary over the years. Holy Name Seminary closed in 1995, the facility became the home of the Diocese of Madison and was named the Bishop O'Connor Catholic Center.

Players and coaches would stay in rooms where the seminarians stayed. There was a large dining area, meeting rooms, large practice fields and areas where the Badger athletic training and strength and conditioning staffs set up. One amenity the facility lacked for the players, however, was air conditioning in the rooms. (The meeting rooms and dining room were air conditioned starting in 1998).

"We had some brutal, hot summer days out there," head coach Barry Alvarez remembered. "The only cool spot sometimes in the summer evenings was the tile floor in the cafeteria, and guys would come down with their pillows and sleep on that tile floor. Just to survive that during those first few years toughened those guys up. It's one of those places where I think anyone who's ever been through this program feels like if you survived that ..."

The Walk-Ons

Head coach Barry Alvarez had seen what the walk-on program had contributed to the University of Nebraska's football program and felt he could do it at Wisconsin, too. He was right.

"I saw Nebraska do it first-hand," Alvarez said of the practice of having non-scholarship players in the program. "They [the Cornhuskers] were the innovator of that, and I just felt like in our situation, with us being the only Division I football school in the state, it gives the athletes in Wisconsin a chance to play football at this level. We've had a lot of success stories. We've had guys come in and end up being NFL players. Every Rose Bowl team we've had has had a walk-on that was a captain."

Among the Badgers' walk-on success stories during Alvarez's tenure are:

• linebacker Bob Adamov, a captain for the 1998 Big Ten and 1999 Rose Bowl championship team;

• linebacker Chad Cascadden, who played for the Badgers' 1993 Big Ten and 1994 Rose Bowl championship team before playing for the New York Jets;

• kicker Matt Davenport, a Lou Groza Award semifinalist and two-time consensus first-team All-Big Ten selection;

• safety Jason Doering, a team captain in 1999 and 2000 and starter on two Big Ten and Rose Bowl championship teams who went on to play in the NFL;

• safety Jim Leonhard, a three-time first-team All-Big Ten choice and first-team Academic All-American, who tied the school record for career interceptions and set the Big Ten record for career punt return yardage;

• offensive tackle Joe Panos, who captained the 1993 Big Ten and 1994 Rose Bowl championship team, was a second-team All-American and played for Philadelphia and Buffalo in the NFL;

• offensive tackle Mark Tauscher, who played for two Big Ten and Rose Bowl championship teams before embarking on a career with the Green Bay Packers;

• linebacker Donnel Thompson, who captained two Big Ten and Rose Bowl championship teams and went on to play in the NFL;

• long snapper Mike Schneck, a member of the 1998 Big Ten and 1999 Rose Bowl championship team, who went on to play for Pittsburgh in the NFL;

• punter Sam Veit, a four-year starter, three-time Academic All-Big Ten selection and member of the 1993 Big Ten and 1994 Rose Bowl championship team.

Entire Unit Drafted

Wisconsin was one of 17 schools in the nation that had at least four players selected in the 2005 National Football League Draft. The Badgers, in fact, had seven players chosen, tying them for the third most in the nation.

Particularly unique for Wisconsin, however, was the fact that its entire starting defensive line was drafted. The four players—ends Erasmus James and Jonathan Welsh, and tackles Jason Jefferson and Anttaj Hawthorne—were key elements on a 2004 Badger defense that ranked sixth nationally in scoring defense and ninth in total defense.

James, a 2004 consensus All-American and the Big Ten Defensive Player of the Year, went to the Minnesota Vikings in the first round with the 18th pick overall. Welsh was a fifth-round choice of the Indianapolis Colts. Hawthorne (Oakland Raiders) and Jefferson (New Orleans Saints) were both sixth-round picks.

Camp Randall Stadium as it looked on September 4, 2004 *Photo by David Stluka*

Renovating Camp Randall

It was 35 years between the addition of an upper deck (1966) and the start of the latest Camp Randall Stadium renovation, but nearly everyone agreed it was worth the wait.

Set for a Grand Re-opening in the fall of 2005, the stadium upgrades made between 2001-2005 gave the legendary facility needed improvements to its infrastructure, as well as aesthetic changes that brought a fresh, new look to the former Civil War training site.

Among the improvements and changes the stadium went through during the most recent renovation were:

• the addition of 72 private suites, 300 premium club seats and 625 club seats

• a new playing surface known as FieldTurf

• new football offices

• a new athletic department office building called Kellner Hall (named for the Kellner family whose lead gift of $10 million—approximately $6.5 million of which went to the stadium renovation—helped the project go forward in 2002 after it was delayed)

• new video scoreboards and a new sound system

• permanent seating in the south end zone that resulted in the addition of 4,432 new seats

• improved and expanded traffic flow in the stadium, along with new concessions and restroom areas

The cost of the entire project was $109 million.